The Nazarene

JAMIE BUCKINGHAM

KINGSWAY PUBLICATIONS
EASTBOURNE

British Library Cataloguing in Publication Data

Buckingham, Jamie
The Nazarene.
I. Title
232.901

ISBN 0-86065-971-2

Printed in Great Britain for
KINGSWAY PUBLICATIONS LTD
1 St Anne's Road, Eastbourne, E. Sussex BN21 3UN by
BPCC Hazell Books, Aylesbury, Bucks.
Reproduced from the original text by arrangement with
Servant Publications

THE NAZARENE

Contents

Introduction

LIFE IS A PILGRIMAGE. Shakespeare said each of us is like a player on a stage, making exits and entrances, playing many different parts. We go, he said, from infant, "mewling and puking in the nurse's arms," to the final stage of second childishness—followed by "mere oblivion."

Looking back I find I have already played many of those parts. I have been infant, child, adolescent, young romantic, husband, father, and now grandfather. But the bard was wrong when he said there was, at the end of the journey, nothing but "mere oblivion." I've written this little book to share with you what I have learned lies ahead. This is a book to help you face life—and death.

The Bible says we are not created to fade into oblivion, but to follow Jesus through the door of death into resurrection life.

Another poet, Henry W. Longfellow, caught that spirit.

Life is real! Life is earnest!
and the grave is not its goal;
Dust thou art, to dust returnest,
Was not spoken of the soul.

I first met the Nazarene through the pages of the Bible. Later, I surrendered my life, as totally as I knew how, to his call. But there remained an emptiness. Jesus was distant. He was a flat picture on the wall. He was a stick figure on a crucifix. He was a fairy-tale character in Sunday school stories. I followed him more out of respect than love.

Then, one night many years ago, during a time of deep personal desperation, Jesus stepped into my life in the presence of his Holy Spirit. In that moment I was immersed, flooded, with the love, grace, and power of his presence. Since then there has been a consuming desire to know him more. I knew I would never be satisfied until I visited the land where he had lived while on earth, walked in his footsteps, and seen this earth through his eyes.

I started my personal pilgrimage to the Holy Land by visiting the Sinai. Over a nine-year period I made seven camping trips into that region described by the Bible as "that great and terrible wilderness." During this time I followed the footsteps of Moses. In order to understand God's grace at Mt. Calvary, I needed to understand God's law at Mt. Sinai.

While exploring the Sinai, I made a number of trips into the land of Israel. The more I visited, the more I developed a love, not only for the people who live there today, but for the land itself—the land of the Bible. Eventually, I stopped my journeys into the Sinai and began to simply follow the footsteps of Jesus through the Holy Land. I had become—and remain—consumed by this man called The Nazarene.

I wanted to see life through his eyes. I wanted to be there, on his turf, so I could understand what he meant when he said such things as "A city set on a hill cannot be hid." I discovered that one evening, sitting on a rock by the lapping waters of the Sea of Galilee. The sun had just gone down behind the Galilean hills. Tiny stars were just beginning to twinkle in the fading sunset. Looking back over my shoulder I saw the flickering lights of the ancient village of Safed, located on the top of a nearby hill, as they blinked on. "A city set on a hill . . ." I understood.

One of these personal pilgrimages was made during Lent—the fifty days before Easter. It was a deeply moving experience. I knew God was calling me to take up my cross also. I made notes during that special Lenten journey in

Israel. Later my friends at Servant Publications asked to publish them. Perhaps my observations would help others who were facing the ultimate question of life: "If a man die, will he live again?"

Then, just as the book was ready for its final editing before printing, something happened to me. I was told by a doctor that I had cancer—and would soon die. The early medical prognosis left no options open. The cancer was "inoperable" and "incurable." Suddenly I found myself in the same position as those people I had written about in the book: the lepers in Galilee, the blind man in Jericho, the cripples on the streets of Jerusalem. These were the helpless ones who held out desperate hands to Jesus and said: "If you are really the Son of God . . ."

I found myself doing what they did, only to discover he not only is still alive—he still answers prayer. What happened to me that summer is the subject of another book. But through a combination of many miracles—occurring over a period of just a few days—the cancer is gone. Jesus of Nazareth is alive—and is still healing helpless people.

The apostle Paul explained it to the church at Ephesus: "I pray that you will begin to understand how incredibly great his power is to help those who believe him. It is that same mighty power that raised Christ from the dead and seated him in that place of honor at God's right hand in heaven.... And God has put all things under his feet..." (Eph 1:19-20, 22 TLB).

As you read this little book I pray you'll not just follow the footsteps of The Nazarene, but you will be so filled with his Holy Spirit that you, too, will experience the miracles of God today.

Jamie Buckingham
Palm Bay, Florida

1

Sunrise in Galilee

"For my Father's will is that everyone who looks to the Son and believes in him shall have eternal life, and I will raise him up at the last day." (Jn 6:40)

L AST NIGHT, just as the Sabbath ended, a great storm whipped across the Sea of Galilee. I stood at the window in my room, watching, the lightning flash and the wind-whipped waves beat on the shore.

I rose early this morning and walked the quiet path through the kibbutz where I spent the night. The slight rosy hue in the eastern sky, outlining the mountains of the misty Golan Heights on the far side of the lake, hinted at dawn's approach. I found this big rock overlooking the water where I could sit and await the sunrise. The water is mirror calm, as though last night's storm never happened.

The quiet of dawn draws my thoughts to God. The night creatures had hushed their soft noises in anticipation of the sun's arrival—much as a theatre audience grows silent just before the curtain is pulled. The only sound was the gentle lapping of the water on the rocks along the shore.

Jesus came here early one morning, many years ago. He too sat on one of these rocks contemplating what his heavenly Father had revealed to him. God wanted Jesus to walk to Jerusalem, a trip he had made several times since leaving his carpenter's job three years earlier.

The rigors of the 90-mile journey did not trouble Jesus— but the purpose did. There, in Jerusalem, he was going to die a horrible death. Yet, even as he sat here and shuddered at the thought of being nailed to a cross, God's Son did not shirk from the call. He knew his father was in control. Jesus also knew, because God had told him, that he would come out of the tomb three days later—opening the door to eternal life for all who believed in him.

My dawn reverie makes me think of death. It is coming to all of us. Yet because of Jesus' death, there is a resurrection for us, too. My heart fills with praise as I sit quietly, looking out over the calm water of this special place.

The ancient Jews called this the Sea of Kinneret from the Hebrew word *kinor*, meaning "harp"—the shape of the lake. The Galilee is more than 600 feet below sea level. Being here this Sunday morning, surrounded by the mountains, is like sitting in the bottom of a giant teacup as the sun rises over the edge.

Sunrise came gradually. The eastern sky began to blush as a bride's cheeks might color in anticipation of the arrival of her new husband.

First the black turned to pink, which was then mixed with streaks of violet changing to light blue. Then the entire horizon, in an instant, was filled with flashes of rose and magenta. Rays of pink and red reflected off the sparse, low clouds which huddled next to the eastern hilltops, as though trying to keep warm in the pre-dawn chill. Finally, just when I was able to pinpoint exactly where the sun would first appear, there was an explosion of brilliant orange and red, heralding the beginning of this new day in Israel.

I sat in silence as the scarlet ball pushed back the darkness, rising like a giant bubble of light out of the indigo night. I could almost see it ascend, gathering speed as it emerged over the dark shadows of the Syrian mountains. Suddenly, it was no longer night—but day.

Now the light revealed the seaside city of Tiberias to my right. Around the bend of the shoreline to the north, the slanting fields on the sides of the Mount of Beatitudes were awash in the morning sun. Tall eucalyptus trees streaked the slopes with shadows.

How many times, I wonder, did the the Son of God sit at this very place and see this same, magnificent sight— watching the sun he created reflect off the sparkling blue water of the Sea of Galilee? Unlike us, Jesus knew his future. Early one morning, sitting near this place, Matthew says "he took the twelve disciples aside and said to them, 'We are going up to Jerusalem, and the Son of Man will be betrayed to the chief priests and the teachers of the law. They will condemn him to death and will turn him over to the Gentiles to be mocked and flogged and crucified. On the third day he will be raised to life!' " (Mt 20:17-19).

The concept was so foreign that the disciples could not understand or even receive it. But Jesus knew—and yet he never flinched from the future. Why? Because he had faith to believe his heavenly Father was in control.

Two fishing boats, nets piled high in the stern, slowly make their way across the sun's brilliant path sparkling on the surface of the water. They've been out all night, dragging their nets, just as the disciples did 2000 years ago. Their wake ripples the path of sunbeams as they chug toward the tiny fishing kibbutz of En Gev on the far side of the lake.

It's springtime here in Galilee. Thanks to the winter rains, the low mountains are awash in vivid color—robed in "the brilliant garb of spring." The field next to me is spotted with vibrant tones—scarlet poppies and yellow and purple blossoms are spread like a colorful quilt over all the pastures of the upper Galilee. Nature is dressing herself to prepare for earth's greatest celebration—Easter Sunday.

In three days Christians around the world will begin the

celebration of Lent. The term "lent" comes from an old English word meaning spring—referring to the brightening or lengthening of the days. This wonderful time of year encompasses the forty weekdays before Easter as a time of repentance and fasting. Ash Wednesday beings this period which symbolizes the forty days Jesus spent in the Judean wilderness following his baptism.

Today is the Sunday the ancient church fathers called *Quinquagayseema,* which heralds the fifty days before Easter. In the liturgy *quinquagayseema* is the first word of the prayer of introduction—called the *introit.* The beginning of the beginning of resurrected life. I hope my lenten visit to the Holy Land will help me understand what Jesus meant when he said, "Because I live, you shall live also."

2

Herald of the Messiah

"I tell you the truth: Among those born of women there has not risen anyone greater than John the Baptist; yet he who is least in the kingdom of heaven is greater than he." (Mt 11:11)

I LOVE THE DESERT—THE SOLITUDE, the dryness, the clear night skies and stark views. The sun was just coming up over the Mountains of Moab as I drove the winding road down from Jerusalem to Jericho. This entire region is called by the ominous name of "the wilderness." Wild and rugged, it is one of the most beautiful desert regions in the world—in its own stark way.

The desert had a wonderful attraction for Jesus, who often pulled aside to spend time alone in quiet places. This was also home for John the Baptist, who lived in one of these caves during his last years.

Just a few miles from here, in 1947, a Bedouin boy was playing with some of his friends. He was throwing stones into some of the ancient caves in the hillside when he heard one of the stones plunk against something. Crawling back into the narrow opening of the cave, the little boy discovered an earthen jar containing one of the most important archaeological finds in 2,000 years. The Dead Sea Scrolls had been preserved in the dry desert air in earthen pots, hidden in the caves. These scrolls preserved huge portions of the Old Testament dating back to the first century.

Jewish archaeologists made a thorough and systematic search of the region where the scrolls were discovered. A nearby hill, or tel, contained the remains of the Essenes, a large group of devout and scholarly people who had lived in seclusion during the time of Christ.

Although their little community lasted only a few generations, their life style was very similar to some of the Christian communities I've visited—both Protestant and Catholic. These people were the forerunners of what the first century Christians later called *koinonia*—family, fellowship, community, the heart of the gathered church.

These Essenes, hungry for God, banded together in the Judean wilderness. They believed only the deeply righteous man was truly free. They formed a brotherhood and lived in their own villages. They farmed, gave themselves to communal study, and worked as scribes copying sacred texts on long leather scrolls. Some of those scrolls, carefully hidden in large urns and sealed to protect them against the elements, had been found by the young Bedouin boy.

Like many who live in today's monasteries or other "vowed" communities, they practiced celibacy, held all property in common, and took care of those among their number who were sick and aged. They were forerunners of today's Jewish kibbutz, although their purpose was different. The Essenes existed for one reason—to prepare for the coming of the Messiah.

By the time Jesus arrived, they numbered almost 4,000. Their largest commune was near the Dead Sea at Qumran. These quiet, devoted men were admitted to the order following a three-year novitiate. Clothed in white robes or habits, they practiced a daily ritual of baptism by immersion, purifying themselves repeatedly for the coming Messiah.

John the Baptist was probably an Essene. Maybe his

elderly parents, Zechariah and Elizabeth, arranged for that before they died. Both knew that John was to be the "forerunner" of the Messiah. It would have been natural for them, as they approached death, to arrange for young John to live with a group of people whose sole purpose on earth was to prepare for the coming of the Son of God.

John, however, had a strong, independent spirit. After living a number of years with the Essenes, he broke from the community. He experienced a strange but powerful stirring in his spirit—a "call" from God to separate himself and move into the wilderness.

To fulfill his role as the last of the Old Testament prophets, John was to live alone, dressed in animal skins. His message: to proclaim not only that the Messiah was coming, but to call people to repentance and cleansing, and to indicate their repentance by being baptized in water. In other words, John the Baptist took the message—and the rite—which had belonged to a small group of people—and gave it to the world.

One day, standing on the banks of the Jordan River where he was preaching and baptizing, John looked up and saw Jesus standing on the far bank. It was a magic moment. For months he had been preaching that the Messiah was coming. Then, standing on the river bank, John looked up and realized: "He is here! The anointed one is here!" His eyes moistened. The one for whom he had so long prepared had at last arrived.

"Behold the Lamb of God," John the Baptist said with choking voice, "who takes away the sin of the world." Immediately Jesus came toward him.

"I've come to be baptized," Jesus said simply.

John objected, then submitted to Jesus' wish.

As Jesus was coming up out of the water, a bright light appeared in the sky. Suddenly a dove descended on Jesus and a voice was heard speaking: "This is my beloved Son in whom I am well pleased."

John's work was finished at that point. Shortly afterwards he was beheaded by King Herod. Jesus said that there was no man, born to a woman, who was held in higher esteem in the eyes of God.

What a marvelous calling: to introduce Jesus to others. We have a similar calling: to introduce the Messiah to the world. Be faithful. No matter how small you think your part.

3

A Place of Rest

"Come to me, all you who are weary and burdened, and I will give you rest." (Mt 11:28)

FAR SOUTH OF JERUSALEM is the Wilderness of Zin, the southernmost region of the Negev Desert. Here the children of Israel wandered for almost forty years following their exodus from Egypt. This wild, barren land lies on the northern border of the Sinai Peninsula. After leaving Mt. Sinai, the huge group of Israelites trudged northward toward the promised land. Their only stop was to be a brief rest at the oasis of Kadesh Barnea.

Moses hadn't intended to stay there long. He was doing with the Israelites what my wife and I used to do with our children when we were traveling in our old station wagon. We'd pull into a service station: "Okay, everyone out for a pottie break." Maybe we'd let them indulge in a soda or crackers. Then back in the car and on the road. We never planned on staying at the service station. It was merely a stop along the way.

Of course it didn't work out that way for Moses and the Israelites. The problem began when Moses sent twelve spies to check out the promised land, then called Canaan. On their return ten of the spies reported the task was im-

19

possible. The cities were all surrounded by high walls. Worse, the land was inhabited by giants.

"We were as grasshoppers to them," the cowardly spies said.

Only two of the twelve—Joshua and Caleb—brought back a positive report.

"The land is flowing with milk and honey," they said. "Sure, there are giants and walled cities—but so what? God told us to take the land and with his help we can do anything."

But the people refused to march forward. As a result God let them wander in the wilderness until the adult population died. Then the new generation of Israelis, following Joshua, entered the promised land and captured it—giants, walled cities, and all.

Along the route from Kadesh Barnea to Canaan is a deep canyon called the Brook Paran—one of the huge dried riverbeds which crosses the Negev Desert in southern Israel. When Moses came through here on his way to the promised land, the children of Israel found *rest* in this place. Ever since then the Brook Paran has been associated with rest. Spiritual rest.

Paran is not really a brook. It's a dried watercourse which in Arabic is called *Wadi Jirafi*, taken from the word "jarafa" which means to wash the soil away. It's a reference to the strong torrents which tear through here during the rainy season causing great soil erosion.

Wadi Paran, then, is a simile of life. At times it is a mad watercourse, a place of unbridled passions and rage. At other times this same place offers ultimate tranquility and solitude. A place of rest.

I'm learning, as I grow older, that God really does understand our life problems. He knows the havoc our passions wreak on our spirit and physical bodies, as well as on the lives of others around us. I guess that's what David meant when he wrote, "Be still, my soul . . ."

God wants us to receive his rest—his peace. This peace that passes all understanding is available to us all, but only as we obey God.

The more I study this land, the more I realize the depth of oppression experienced by the people of Jesus' day. Apart from Roman domination, the Jewish law itself was impossible to keep. The Jews lived under constant condemnation. To those people—as to us—Jesus said, "Come to me, all you who are weary and burdened, and I will give you rest. Take my yoke upon you and learn from me, for I am gentle and humble in heart, and you will find rest for your souls. For my yoke is easy and my burden is light" (Mt 11:28-30).

God never intended earth to be our final destination. Earth is just a brief rest stop on the way to the Promised Land. Fools don't understand this, and live their lives as if earth were home. But earth is not home. This world is not a place to build bigger and better barns or to lay up goods where thieves break in and steal. Earth is but a preparation for what is yet to come—God's glorious promised land of heaven. All the more reason we should enjoy our stay and not be anxious—no matter how grim the situation. God has a better place prepared for us.

Not far from here, near the Dead Sea, is a marvelous canyon with a constant running stream called En Gedi. Surrounded by desert mountains, in the bottom of this steep ravine, is a stream of pure water—coming from a hidden waterfall at the far end of the canyon, or wadi. It was there David wrote that wonderful poem we now call Psalm 23, a song of rest.

The LORD is my shepherd; I shall not want.
He maketh me to lie down in green pastures:
He leadeth me beside the still waters.
He restoreth my soul . . .

Rest and peace . . . even in the midst of conflict.

> Yea, though I walk through the valley
>   of the shadow of death,
> I will fear no evil:
> For thou art with me;
> Thy rod and thy staff they comfort me. . . .

Rest and peace, even in the presence of death.

> Thou preparest a table before me in the presence
>   of mine enemies:
> Thou anointest my head with oil;
> my cup runneth over. . . . (KJV)

Rest and peace in the midst of torment, passion, and fear. Here quietness abounds in the presence of Jesus, who brings the peace that passes understanding.

Susanna Wesley, the mother of John and Charles, had nineteen children. When they became too much for her, she would stand in the middle of her kitchen, reach down and pull her long skirt up over head and hold it closed with her hand. This became her "prayer closet." There in the place of turmoil, she found rest.

4

"God, Be Merciful to Me, a Sinner"

"He mocks proud mockers but gives grace to the humble."

(Prv 3:34)

E ACH OF US HAS OUR OWN WAY OF APPROACHING GOD. I've seen a lot of that here in Israel, which is an incredible salad of Judaism and Islam, mixed in with representatives of every church group in the world. Most incredible, everyone here—including myself—says he knows the proper way to God.

Actually, there's only one way to God. The Bible is the map of the road we must follow. Once we depart from it, the paths go off in every conceivable direction. Sadly, most of those paths lead straight to despair, deceit, and destruction. Others come so close to the flames you can't help getting singed.

The apostle Paul said one determining factor separates Christians from everyone else: we believe in the bodily resurrection of Christ from the dead. Without the resurrection, Christianity is nothing more than a wonderful set of moral laws. But if Christ arose, and if he lives in our hearts, then all else fades into insignificance.

23

Early this morning I got up and walked through the awakening streets of Jerusalem. A month before Passover, the shops are already advertising. I made my way into a small Catholic church near the wall of the Old City. Even though I'm not Catholic, I had a strong desire to pause this morning, on a day the church world calls "Ash Wednesday," and join with millions around the world preparing for Easter.

Preparation to meet God must always begin with repentance: a genuine turning away from the things that displease God in order to turn to him with clean hands and a pure heart.

I knelt at the altar of the little church. Less than a dozen people were present for the early morning service. The priest, speaking with a French accent, invited us to "the observance of a holy Lent, by self-examination and repentance; by prayer, fasting, and self-denial; by reading and meditation on God's holy word, to make a right beginning of repentance."

Then, as we knelt at the altar, the priest touched our foreheads with the ashes from the burned palm fronds used during last year's Palm Sunday. Ashes are the symbol of repentance. The symbol of humility. The symbol of fasting and praying.

Yet as I emerged from the church into the bright light of Jerusalem, I was glad I had not waited until Ash Wednesday to repent. There is a difference, I've discovered, between fasting and living the fasted life. As important as it is to fast on regular occasions, the fasted life means we live constantly in a state of humbling ourselves before men and repenting before God.

Now it's noon and the sun is directly overhead—hot and direct. I'm sitting on the wall of a small parapet overlooking the western wall of the old temple. I am aware that the dot of ash is still on my forehead and wonder if the people passing by wonder about it. Looking at the Jews coming and going, pausing at the wall and praying, I wonder how many times during his brief life on earth Jesus came to this same place in the Holy City.

Jerusalem is the most resilient city in the world. Across the centuries it has been under siege many times. On several occasions it was totally destroyed. The temple itself was destroyed twice—and rebuilt.

Sitting here, looking at the shadows play on the huge white stones of the wall, the lessons of history race through my mind. Solomon first built the temple more than 900 years before Christ. It stood for 400 years before being destroyed by the Babylonians. The temple was rebuilt by Zerubbabal when the Jews returned from exile, but ravaged again by the Syrians and Romans before Christ was born. Rebuilt again by King Herod, it was finally destroyed by the Romans in A.D. 70. The Jews were scattered throughout the earth.

During that 2,000 year period—a time called the diaspora—the Moslems moved into Jerusalem. In 691 they built a huge Moslem shrine—called the Mosque of Omar—right on the Temple Mount next to where the original Jewish temple once stood. Next to it stands the famous Dome of the Rock, its magnificent golden dome still dominating the skyline of Jerusalem.

The only part of the original temple which remains today is this small portion of the western wall, which the Jews call the Wailing Wall.

For Christians the temple has many meanings, perhaps none better captured than in one of the parables Jesus told. Two men, he said, came to the temple to pray. One, a Pharisee, came to show off his religion. He came to brag about the money he gave, about his piousness, about his weekly fasting.

The other man, a miserable tax collector, was too ashamed to pray out loud. He merely knelt off to one side—weeping. "God have mercy on me, a sinner," he whispered in his pain.

The Pharisees loved to brag about their fasting. They put

white powder in their hair and on their faces to indicate how pious they were. Jesus, however, pointed out that it was the sinner who knelt in deep repentance who was blessed by God—and returned to his house forgiven.

True repentance is not just a spot of ashes on my forehead, but a heart that weeps over its sinfulness and cries out in anguish, "God, be merciful to me, a sinner."

Jesus said in the Sermon on the Mount: "When you fast, do not look somber as the hypocrites do, for they disfigure their faces to show men they are fasting. I tell you the truth, they have received their reward in full. But when you fast, put oil on your head and wash your face, so that it will not be obvious to men that you are fasting, but only to your Father, who is unseen; and your Father, who sees what is done in secret, will reward you" (Mt 6:16-18).

The one thing we don't want to do is become proud of our humility.

5

A Land of Conflict

"...just as Christ was raised from the dead through the glory of the Father, we too may live a new life." (Rom 6:4)

ISRAEL HAS BEEN A LAND OF STRIFE AND CONFLICT since the days of Abraham. No other nation in history has been through as many wars, suffered under as many occupations, seen as much grief and bloodshed as this tiny nation.

Last night I was in Jerusalem at the western wall—sometimes known as the Wailing Wall. Jesus must have been there many times. Not at that wall, for it was but the outside wall of the rampart around the old temple. But he would have passed by, and would have walked on those stones. As the orthodox Jews of today come to the wall, Jesus made regular visits to the temple, praying David's prayer for the peace of Jerusalem: "May there be peace within your walls and security within your citidels."

Last night, wearing the traditional yarmulke on my head, I stood quietly at the wall and prayed that same prayer. I also asked God to reveal the true Messiah to the people of this nation. Only then will real peace come.

Leaving the wall I stopped to talk to an old Jewish rabbi. He was deeply burdened about the terrible conflict this nation continues to experience. Being Jewish, he talked about the persecution the Jews have endured over the centuries. Tears came to his eyes and he slowly shook his head. "Such is the price of being 'chosen,'" he said. "The world hates us—just as the brothers of Joseph hated him simply because God had chosen him to lead."

He then told me of a beautiful Jewish tradition. "Once a year," he said, "in the dead of night on the eve of Tisha be-Av, the day we Jews believe both the first and second temples were destroyed, a white dove—the symbol of Divine Presence—appears and coos sadly with the mourners at the wall as they stand, praying and weeping.

"At night," the rabbi continued solemnly, "the stones are covered with drops of dew which are the tears the Wailing Wall sheds while weeping with all Israel over the continued conflict between God's people."

What a beautiful legend. No one really believes it, but it perfectly illustrates the sadness felt by Jews worldwide over their persecution—and the grave problems that exist between the Jews and other Semitic peoples—for whom Christ also died.

That sadness is shared, not just by the Jews, but by the others who occupy this little land. The Palestinian people—remnants of those who lived here before the Jews moved back home in 1948, are also victims of the violence. These people, once brothers, now struggle to live side-by-side without killing each other. The struggle has not always been successful. Someone has to rule. The ruler is always looked upon as the oppressor, the ruled as the aggressor.

Last week a bomb exploded on a city bus in Jericho—killing a young Jewish mother and her two small children. The police said the bomb had been placed in a shoe box and left under the seat.

Yesterday reports of more violence came from the village of Nablus in the West Bank. Nablus is on the site of the ancient city of Shechem, the old capital of Samaria in the days of Jesus. Even then it was a place of violence. Jews were afraid to go through Samaria for fear of being stoned. Orthodox Jews, if they caught a Samaritan away from home, might stone him. Jesus made constant reference to the Samaritans—pointing out they were "our neighbors" who were to be loved as we love ourselves. It was a Samaritan leper, one of 10 Jews and Samaritans who had the disease who alone returned to Jesus to give thanks for his healing.

Today the same conflict, the same weapons, are in use as Palestinians stone Jews and Jewish soldiers respond with swift, harsh, often fatal retaliation. No one wins.

Today I'm sitting quietly in one of the great forests planted by a group of Christians who are helping Israel reforest the land. Off to my right is a reddish brown area where a forest fire, set by terrorists, raged through here recently. The fire burned a section of trees that took thirty-five years to grow—and will take another thirty-five years to replace.

Across the centuries this land had been raped by pagans and Christians alike. The Turks, for instance, cut down every tree in the nation during their occupation. In 1948, when the Jews returned, they started the long, tedious process of reforestation. Slowly, the land began to turn from brown to green as hundreds of thousands of acres of forest appeared.

The words of Job were fulfilled: "There is hope for a tree: If it is cut down, it will sprout again, and its new shoots will not fail. Its roots may grow old in the ground and its stump die in the soil, yet at the scent of water it will bud and put forth shoots like a plant" (Jb 14:7-9).

As the trees grew, another wonderful phenomenon took place. The leaves of the trees gave off oxygen into the air. The oxygen mixed with the hydrogen in the air and formed rain clouds. The entire climate of the nation changed. Rain, which had not fallen in centuries, once again pelted the formerly scorched earth. The mountains and the hills, once barren sand and rock, turned green with grass and flowers.

The prophecies of Isaiah came to pass: "The desert and the parched land will be glad; the wilderness will rejoice and blossom. Like the crocus, it will burst into bloom . . ." (Is 35:1-2).

Then the terrorists struck, setting forest fires. Thousands of acres of beautiful Jerusalem pine were turned to charred trunks and gray ash.

With the exception of the Jordan River—fed by the snow on Mt. Hermon and the Sea of Galilee—and a few springs along the coast, Israel depends on water from the heavens—water which is placed there by the oxygen breathed off by the trees. Trees cause rain. Rain nourishes trees. Without trees there is no rain.

As today's terrorists have tried to destroy the nation of Israel by burning its trees, so two thousand years ago Satan tried to stop the Messiah from saving the world by having him nailed to a cross.

But just as new growth springs from this scorched earth—so the Messiah could not be held in a tomb. He rose from the grave and has given to us the gift of eternal life—fulfilling another prophecy from Isaiah: "In days to come . . . Israel will bud and blossom and fill all the world with fruit" (Is 27:6).

6

Two Kings

"Where is the one who has been born king of the Jews? We saw his star in the east and have come to worship him." When King Herod heard this he was disturbed. . . . (Mt 2:2–3)

WHILE THE WORLD'S SYSTEMS are dominated by powerful—and sometimes cruel—men, God alone controls history. In the end it is his love and kindness which rules the world, not hatred and selfish greed.

Early this morning I climbed the steep path up a high, man-made mountain south of Bethlehem. Inside the mountain, shaped like the cone of a volcano, are the ancient ruins of the palace of one of those powerful and cruel men—a man who called himself Herod the Great. The place is called the Herodium.

The morning is cold and the wind is blowing. The chill, however, is more than what I feel on my skin. There is a heart-chill here, for this was the home of one of the cruelest men of history.

Herod's palace was located on this high plateau. However, when he chose this spot for his palatial residence, the plateau was only half the height it is today. Jewish slaves, many of whom died and were buried where they fell, brought the rest of the dirt and rock in by hand.

The Herodium was a magnificent palace with towers, colonnaded courtyards, baths, and decorations to match anything Caesar had built in Rome. Two hundred marble steps ascended to it. But it was a monument to cruelty—and to a man who tried to change history with hate and fear. So, despite the former beauty of this palace, I cannot forget the high price paid in human suffering for one man's selfish, egotistic comfort.

Herod was a puppet governor under the Romans with no real authority. That was held only by the Roman occupiers. But he was granted unlimited funds and allowed to collect taxes by any means he chose. He was expected by the Romans to do one thing—keep the people under control. Herod accomplished this with cruelty and intimidation. During his reign this wicked king ordered the death of tens of thousands of innocent people—including thousands of infants and children.

Yet only a few miles from here, in a lowly cave behind a small inn, another king was born. His mission on earth was to give his life for the sake of suffering humanity. He came to redeem all who were poor, forsaken, lonely, and oppressed.

Herod built his palace for one reason—to satisfy himself. It was of no importance for defense or trade. A renegade Jew, he had enjoyed an early life of luxury in the Greek-Roman world in which he had found his niche. Herod made a pretense of being religious—rebuilding the great temple in Jerusalem. But like his palace, it also was built with slave labor at the expense of thousands of lives.

Like many wealthy men of power, Herod was unhappy. He was overweight, obese. He had trouble sleeping, had nightmares, and was tormented with demons. Herod was so suspicious of his own family that he often disguised himself at night, sneaking through his palace to spy on his own children and grandchildren. When anyone threatened him, even his own family, he had them executed. Herod feared

God, but did not serve or worship him. This miserable man was never at peace with himself.

On the other hand, Jesus had nothing of this world's goods. He lived in borrowed houses. He owned nothing except his robe—which was a gift. Yet he had everything. Jesus was a man of peace and love, totally content.

Herod had no regard for human life. People, as he saw them, were on earth for one purpose—to serve him. Jesus, on the other hand, said he had come to serve people—not for them to serve him.

It's difficult to imagine a greater contrast than the one between Herod and Jesus. Herod had all the attributes Jesus ascribed to Satan. He was a liar and a murderer. The wise men, following the star, stopped at the Herodium and told Herod they were looking for the Christ-child. Herod called his scholars. "Yes," they agreed, "the prophet Micah prophesied the Messiah would be born in nearby Bethlehem."

Bethlehem. I spent yesterday evening there. Just as the sun was going down I sat in a quiet pasture watching two Arab shepherd boys drawing water from an ancient well and pouring it in a stone trough. Very little has changed there since Jesus was born near that field. It was there the star came and shone on the manger bed. The shepherds heard the angels and sought out the straw birthing bed in the stable.

How different from the bed of gold and ivory where Herod lay each night in his Herodium, tossing and screaming through his demon-possessed nightmares.

Herod told the wise men, "Go and make a careful search for the child. As soon as you find Him, report to me, so that I, too, may go and worship Him." Warned in a dream, the wise men returned to their eastern land by another route, Herod grew furious. He ordered his soldiers to kill all the boy babies in Bethlehem and the vicinity.

That night Joseph had a dream. Waking, he took Mary and

the baby and fled to Egypt where they waited until Herod died.

Archaeologists believe the bones of the old king are here—buried by his equally wicked sons. Historians tell us Herod died a horrible death. Now they can't even find his bones. His remains, like his evil works, have disappeared.

Two kings.
Herod the Great.
Jesus the Servant.
One ruled as tyrant—and died as he lived,
   in fear and terror.
The other was willing to be crucified,
   giving his life as a ransom for many.
One is virtually forgotten.
   His only memorial is this dusty ruin.
The other reigns today in the hearts of millions
   all over the world—the King of Kings
   and Lord of Lords.

7

Demons Flee in His Name

... Resist the devil, and he will flee from you. (Jas 4:7)

I GOT UP EARLY THIS MORNING and walked south along the eastern shore of the Sea of Galilee to where I am right now—sitting on a big rock at the foot of a high bluff. The beach is covered with small round stones, eroded from the high bluffs which extend up to the Golan Heights.

Almost two thousand years have passed since Jesus visited this region—then called the Decapolis because of the ten Greek cities located in the area. One of them was a village called Gadara. The hills have been eroded by wind and rain and a hundred armies have marched back and forth over this land. But the place remains much the same.

It's almost noon. I've been sitting in the shadow of this cliff for almost an hour. Jesus and his disciples once beached their fishing boat one night and then climbed this cliff. On top they met a demon-possessed man in a graveyard. What followed was a powerful confrontation between the Son of God and the demons of hell.

Earlier this morning I walked along the top of the cliff. I wanted to walk out to the edge and look over, but my way was blocked by two rows of rusted barbed wire, placed there by the Israeli army following the 1967 war with Syria. Before pulling out the Syrians had placed land mines all along the cliff top. International signs for land mines posted on the rusting fence—a red triangle on a yellow field—warn people like me that the cliff top remains an active mine field.

Since the time of Jesus this area has been a war zone. Yet while many men have fought and died in this region, there have been other battles just as real going on in the "heavenly" regions. These are the battles for the souls of men; for this place remains, as it was in Jesus' day, a haven for demons.

On the cliff top Jesus had a frightening encounter with a man who was possessed with so many demons they called themselves "legion"—after the Roman army division of 6,000.

It's an incredible story. Thousands of demons—like bees swarming in a hollow tree stump—had taken up residence in a local citizen and driven him to madness. The people of Gadara, afraid of the man, had chained him to a tree. But with superhuman strength he had broken the chains and fled to that ancient cemetery where he lived in the caves and wandered around the above-ground tombs.

That night when Jesus came ashore he climbed this cliff with his small group of followers. In order to get to Gadara they had to pass through the cemetery. While some of the dead were buried in the caves, most dead bodies were laid on top of the ground and covered with stones. The men were gingerly making their way through the piles of stones when suddenly, leaping from behind one of the graves, came this crazed, demon-possessed man. Screaming like a banshee, he ran toward them, broken chains flapping from his wrists and ankles, his arms flailing, his hair flying behind him. He was totally naked, his body dripping blood where he had deliberately cut himself with sharp stones.

Suddenly the demons recognized they were face to face

with the Son of God. Jesus rebuked them and they swarmed into a nearby herd of pigs. The now possessed swine stampeded over the cliff into the sea where they drowned.

An incredible story, but no more incredible than the things taking place today as God's people once again take authority over demons in the name of Jesus. At a recent Sunday morning worship service in our church, the congregation was standing, praising God. Suddenly a woman began to shriek and scream. Invited by a friend, it was her first visit to our church. Both ladies were wealthy members of elite community organizations.

But as the congregation began to enter into worship, the demons inside her broke loose with all of hell's fury. She staggered out into the aisle, frothing at the mouth, flailing her arms and shrieking nonsense and obscenities. One of our pastors stepped out in front of her and commanded the demons, in the name of Jesus, to leave. Instantly the woman collapsed into the aisle. Several people knelt and ministered to her while the rest of the church kept on singing and praising God. Within moments she was free. The demons were gone. The woman had been delivered.

In Jesus Christ we have power and authority over all evil spirits. The apostle Paul, who had his own fights with demons, pointed out that even though Jesus defeated Satan at the cross, the battle still rages. However, it is not against flesh and blood, but against the rulers, against the authorities, against the powers of this dark world and against the spiritual forces of evil in heavenly realms. The victory, however, has already been won at Calvary.

I was only 12 years old when the Americans crossed the English Channel in World War II and landed on the beaches of Normandy. The code name given to that day by General Eisenhower was D-Day. We had invaded Europe and the victory was assured from that point. But the war was not over. There was much fighting to be done. It wasn't until V-Day, more than a year later, that ultimate victory was

assured and the enemy laid down their arms in unconditional surrender.

Calvary was our D-Day. The return of Jesus will be V-Day.
Until then, there are many spiritual battles to be fought. But
the victory is assured. Even though we may get battered
around, we have full authority over the enemy. Speak the
name of Jesus—and demons flee. Resist the devil, and he will
flee from you. That's the message from Gadara.

Although the Bible says Satan is a roaring lion seeking
whom he may devour, his teeth were pulled at Calvary.
Despite what you may have read, Satan is not alive and well
on planet Earth. He is alive, but mortally wounded. All who
believe in Jesus have authority over him. Resist him in Jesus'
name, and he will flee from you.

8

Angels

Then the devil left him, and angels came and attended him.

(Mt 4:11)

IT'S IMPOSSIBLE TO THINK OF THE TIME Jesus spent on earth without thinking about the angels that constantly surrounded him, ministering to him, protecting him.

In this shepherd's field outside Bethlehem, where I am today, the greatest angel visitation known to man took place. The skies were full of them—from horizon to horizon, heralding the birth of the Messiah.

But the angels in Jesus' life went back earlier than his birth. Fifteen months before the birth of Christ, an angel appeared to an old Jewish priest named Zechariah who was ministering in the temple in Jerusalem. "Do not be afraid, Zechariah, your prayer has been heard. Your wife Elizabeth will bear you a son, and you are to give him the name John." He became known as John the Baptist.

Six months following, ninety miles north in the little town of Nazareth, another angel, Gabriel, appeared to a simple teenage girl named Mary. "Hail," the angel said, "thou that art highly favoured, the Lord is with thee: blessed art thou among women."

Nine months later, in this same field where I'm standing, "Shepherds were abiding in the field, keeping watch over their flock by night. And, lo, the angel of the Lord came upon them, and the glory of the Lord shone round about them ..."

I memorized those words as a child—along with all those wonderful Christmas carols about angels.

"Angels from the realms of glory ..."
"Hark, the herald angels sing ..."
"While shepherds watched their flocks by night,
    all seated on the ground,
    the angel of the Lord came down, and
    glory shone around...."

The Bible says the angels which sang over this field "returned to heaven." But not for long, for they continued to make appearances throughout the life of Jesus.

Now, as we approach the end of the age, angel appearances are once again taking place. From all over the world come reports of angel sightings. That's not surprising.

The term angel—"angelos" in Greek—means simply "messenger." They are God's "special delivery" messengers. They seem to take on many shapes and forms. Sometimes angels appear as heavenly beings. At other times, they appear in human form. Paul warns us to be careful about turning away strangers, lest we turn away an angel unawares.

Some angels minister to God around his throne. Others minister to us on earth—especially to those who have great needs.

A respected Episcopal priest told me of the time a man stopped by his church to ask for prayer before entering the hospital. He had just received word he was going blind. Together they entered the empty, semi-dark sanctuary where the man knelt at the altar. As they prayed, the priest looked up. There, hovering around the kneeling man, were dozens of small angels ministering to him. The next day the doctors sent the man home from the hospital. They could find no trace of the earlier disease. He was healed.

After Jesus had been tempted by Satan in the Judean wilderness, just a few miles from here, the Bible says the angels came and ministered to him.

The night before Jesus was crucified, he came to the Garden of Gethsemane to pray. He sweated blood in the intense prayer of agony. Physically and emotionally exhausted, Jesus leaned against a huge rock and an angel from heaven came and strengthened him.

Angels rolled away the stone from the grave of Jesus the morning of his resurrection. Then they waited for first light and spoke to the women who came to anoint his body. "Why do you seek the living among the dead? He is risen!"

Finally, angels surrounded him on the Mount of Olives as he ascended into heaven following his resurrection. Turning to those who stood looking, they said, "This same Jesus, who has been taken from you into heaven, will come back in the same way you have seen him go into heaven."

It all began in this rock strewn field outside the village of Bethlehem. God continues to send his messengers—and his warriors—to aid his people in the battles of these last days. Keep your eyes and ears open for angels. God may have a special message—just for you.

9

Victory over Temptation

"Jesus was led up by the Spirit into the wilderness. . . ."

(Mt 4:1, NKJV)

THE WILDERNESS. The very term causes us to shudder. Here in Israel the wilderness is real, not just a word in the Bible, or a phrase preachers use to describe a tough time in our pilgrimage through life.

Overlooking the city of Jericho is an ancient and almost inaccessible Greek Monastery—called the Monastery of the Forty Days. Clinging precariously to the cliff 1,000 feet above the Jordan Valley, its bells can be heard across the plain of Jericho. The Romans called this mountain *Mons Quarantanta*—Mount of the Forty. Today's Arabs call it *Quarantal*.

The old Greek monk, whom I have met several times before, let me through the front door after he heard my knock. Walking before me in silence, his long black robe swished across the stone floor of the narrow corridor. He padded softly through the old monastery, out onto the wobbly balcony which extends over the nothingness of space, and then to the back door which he unlocked. I pointed at my watch and held up four fingers to let him know I would be back in four hours. Expressionless, the

42

monk motioned me through, closing the door behind me. I heard the iron latch fall into place, where it will remain until I knock, asking to pass back through so I can climb back down the mountain to my car.

Climbing higher than the belfrey which dominates the steeple, I labored up the steep path to the summit—another 1,000 feet above the monastery. Now I sit here, watching the ravens ride the thermals below me, looking at the meandering Jordan River as it sluggishly makes it's way south to the Dead Sea. I've been listening to the moans of the desert wind over the barren rocks of this forsaken mountain peak. I am alone—in the wilderness—much as Jesus was.

This is the bleakest place in all Israel. Yet it was here, in this Judean wilderness, that Jesus came following his baptism in the River Jordan. Satan appeared, tempting him to redirect his ministry from the spiritual kingdom of God to a kingdom of materialism, power, and magic.

Somewhere on this mountain behind me—now called the Mount of Temptation—the greatest battle of history took place. Not combat between flesh and blood, between opposing armies or armed warriors. But a battle in the spirit realm—between the two most powerful forces in the universe: the source of evil, known as Satan, and the commander in chief of the Lord's host, the Son of God.

That battle was won by Jesus Christ, but skirmishes continue to this day. On one side is Satan and his countless demons. On the other side is Jesus and his angels. The battle is for the bodies and souls of men and women on earth.

Today, 2,000 years after Satan and Jesus came face to face on this mountain, the area still reeks of Satan's presence. The earth, as though scorched by the conflict, remains scarred. Nothing grows here. No one lives here. It is a place of devastation, for here Satan, attempting to destroy Jesus, was defeated as Jesus quoted the Word of God. Withdrawing, he spit upon the earth. From that time on nothing has grown here. The wilderness is an apt name indeed.

Jesus came here to fast and pray—to prepare for his public ministry on earth. After he was alone for forty days, Satan confronted Him—tempting him in three areas.

"You're hungry," Satan observed. "Turn these rocks into bread. That way you can not only fill your own stomach but feed all the starving people on earth." Jesus fought off the temptation to form a kingdom based on materialism and good works. He quoted Scripture back to Satan: "Man does not live by bread alone."

Next Satan tempted Jesus with power. Taking him to a high place, Satan showed him in an instant all the kingdoms of the world. "I am the prince of this world," Satan said. "It belongs to me. I will give it all to you if you will worship me." Again Jesus fought him off using the Bible: "It is written; 'Worship the Lord your God and serve him only.' "

Finally, Satan led Jesus to Jerusalem and had him stand on the highest point of the temple. That spot is still here, on the outer wall of the old city, called "the pinnacle of the temple." "If you are the Son of God, throw yourself off," Satan tempted. Then he, too, quoted Scripture from Psalm 91: "For it is written, he will command his angels concerning you to guard you carefully. They will lift you up . . ."

Jesus refused to build a kingdom on magic. His eyes must have blazed when he quoted back from the Torah "Do not put the Lord your God to the test" (Dt 6:16). The battle was over. Satan fled and angels came to minister to Jesus.

Satan did not try to kill Jesus—just turn him from his mission. Satan knew death could not stop Jesus. The only thing that could stop him was sin—to cause him to miss the mark of establishing his kingdom on earth. Jesus emerged victorious—and went ahead to do the one thing Satan feared most—die for our sins. That death, and the resurrection which followed, is the culmination of spiritual victory.

Jesus is still victorious. Satan is real. Demons are real. But praise God, "greater is he that is in you than he that is in the world." We can take authority over the dark forces that seek to control our lives and the lives of our loved ones. When we rebuke Satan in the name of Jesus, he flees.

10

The Messiah

> ... *"Are you the one who was to come, or should we expect someone else?"* (Mt 11:3)

OF ALL THE PROPHECIES OF THE OLD TESTAMENT, none is stronger than those saying God was going to send his Messiah to earth. Messiah, in Hebrew, means "anointed one."

Messiah is a precious word to us, as well as to the Jews. That same word when translated into Greek is *Christos*. While the Jews still await the long-expected Messiah, millions of Christians believe that Jesus of Nazareth is the anointed one.

As a child I thought Jesus' last name was Christ. I later discovered Christ was a title, not a name. Jesus was a common name, like John or Jim. To distinguish him from other men named Jesus, he was known as Jesus of Nazareth. Usually men were identified as the son of their father. Simon (later called Peter) was officially known as Simon bar Jonah; or "Simon son of Jonah."

Jesus, however, was never called *Jesus bar Joseph*. He was not the son of Joseph. He was the Son of God, conceived by the Holy Spirit in a virgin maid from Nazareth. Therefore, his followers simply combined the name of Jesus with his title.

46

Following his resurrection, he became known as Jesus Christ—Jesus the Anointed One. The Messiah.

To the Jews the Messiah was the expected king and deliverer of the Hebrews, who would free them from the yoke of aliens and make them a great nation ruling over the whole earth.

This afternoon I climbed to the summit of Mt. Meron, 3,962 feet, the highest in Israel. Located between Haifa and the Sea of Galilee, its peak is easily seen for miles around.

Mt. Meron is important to the Jews because a famous rabbi, Shim'on bar Yahov, who lived in the second century, is buried on the mountainside. He is buried next to his son, Eleazar, also a distinguished rabbi. Hundreds of Jews come to these tombs to pray, believing this to be a sacred spot. In the same building is a yeshiva, a seminary where young men come to study to be rabbis.

As I was visiting the tomb of Rabbi Shim'on, I heard singing outside in the courtyard. A family of Moroccan Jews—four generations of them—had gathered to celebrate a miracle. When one of the men was miraculously healed of a serious kidney disease, they fulfilled their promise to God by holding a day-long family celebration at the tomb of Rabbi Shim'on.

When the family saw me they insisted I join the celebration as an honored guest. Before I knew it, I was laughing, eating, drinking, and singing along with them—celebrating with joy and thanksgiving the miracle of healing. They handed me a huge plate loaded down with food—roast lamb cooked on an open grill, baked chicken, corn, millet, salad, falafel, humus.

One thing was evident: when Jews celebrate a miracle they hold nothing back. It made me wonder what would happen if my Christian friends back home entered into thanksgiving and celebration with as much gusto and joy.

My primary reason for visiting the mountain was not the tombs of the rabbis, however. Rather I came to see this rock where I'm now sitting. Perched on the mountainside, the early rabbis called it "The Throne of Messiah." When the Messiah comes, the rabbis said, he will first appear sitting on this rock. Then Elijah the prophet would appear and blow a trumpet to herald the deliverance of all Israel.

Standing close by is an ancient, free-standing doorway—all that remains of the central door of the Synagogue of Meron, built during the second century. This doorway is made of two huge stones upon which rests the upper lintel—a third massive stone laid across the two vertical doorposts. The lintel is cracked and looks as though it might fall at any moment. The old rabbis said if it should fall of its own accord, it would mark the coming of the Messiah. (Ironically, if you walk through the weeds around to the back side of the doorway you'll discover the lintel has been braced with a large slab of steel. It was put there after it cracked to keep it from falling.)

Most Jews believed the Messiah would come as a thundering prophet like Jeremiah. Others thought he would be another Moses, or perhaps a military leader like Judas the Maccabee, who 200 years before with his small band of Jewish zealots had defeated the mighty Syrian army.

Jesus' disciples struggled with these concepts. As the time for his crucifixion grew near, they gradually began to realize that Jesus was not the kind of Messiah the rabbis had told them to expect. Instead of a militant king, he had come as a suffering servant.

Not until after his resurrection did they fully recognize him for who he was . . . and is. Jesus is the Anointed One in whom lies all the power and authority of God. That power and authority has now been granted to us by the gift of his Holy Spirit. All we need to do is accept. And stand.

11

Salt and Light

"You are the salt of the earth. . . . You are the light of the world. . . ." (Mt 5:13–14)

NOT LONG AFTER JESUS called his disciples, he walked around the shore of the Sea of Galilee and stopped on the north side at the base of this mountain. I've been here since early morning, listening to a flock of nearby sheep letting their shepherd know it's time to head out to the lush mountainside pasture.

A large crowd of people had gathered to hear Jesus speak that morning long ago. They had also come to see him perform healing miracles, and to perhaps receive one themselves. They came from all the surrounding villages— Capernaum, Bethsaida, Tiberias, Magdala.

This slope is called the Mount of Beatitudes. Behind me is a beautiful Catholic church, sitting quietly in a garden-like atmosphere. To my left is an orange grove in full bloom, the perfume of its blossoms filling the air. Stretching out before me is the beautiful, blue Sea of Galilee.

Jesus went up on a mountainside to escape the crushing crowd. Perhaps it was right here, on this very rock, that he sat down and rested. His disciples followed him. As the sun rose higher over the peaceful countryside, Jesus turned to his friends and began to teach them about the kingdom of God. That teaching was beautifully recorded by Matthew and is now called "The Sermon on the Mount."

The passage, as recorded in Matthew 5-7, begins with what is known as the "beatitudes." The word is translated "blessed" in many versions of the Bible, but a better translation is "happy." Sitting here on the side of the mountain—watching the flowers on the hillside bend before the gentle breeze, the sheep contentedly graze, the picturesque lake sparkle in the background—I can almost sense Jesus' presence. Matthew captures the moment in his biography.

> Now when he saw the crowds, he went up on a mountainside and sat down. His disciples came to him, and he began to teach them, saying:
>
> "Blessed are the poor in spirit,
>   for theirs is the kingdom of heaven.
> Blessed are those who mourn,
>   for they will be comforted.
> Blessed are the meek,
>   for they will inherit the earth.
> Blessed are those who hunger and thirst for righteousness,
>   for they will be filled.
> Blessed are the merciful,
>   for they will be shown mercy.
> Blessed are the pure in heart,
>   for they will see God.
> Blessed are the peacemakers,
>   for they will be called sons of God.
> Blessed are those who are persecuted because of righteousness,
>   for theirs is the kingdom of heaven.
> Blessed are you when people insult you, persecute you and falsely say all kinds of evil against you because of me.

Rejoice and be glad, because great is your reward in heaven, for in the same way they persecuted the prophets who were before you." Mt 5:1-12

The beatitudes seemed a strange introduction to his ministry on earth. The disciples had already seen him work miracles. In fact, the verses just before this say that Jesus went throughout Galilee, teaching in the synagogues, preaching the good news of the kingdom, and healing every disease and sickness among the people. News about him had spread all over the area. People brought to him all who were ill with various diseases, those suffering severe pain, the demon-possessed, those having seizures and the paralyzed—and Jesus healed them.

Perhaps the disciples felt they were about to be catapulted into a powerful ministry of healing and deliverance. Riding the messianic coattails of Jesus, each one of them would become world famous. Before their egos got too big, Jesus pulled them aside and began to teach them what the kingdom of God was all about: service to others, comfort, meekness, righteousness, mercy, peace, and persecution.

Persecution is not a popular word, then or now. But a true follower of Jesus Christ will always be misunderstood by the world. Why? Because he is different. That, in essence, is what it means to be holy. It means to be like God, who is different from all others.

As the disciples began to open their food bags and pull out the salted fish they would eat for supper, Jesus said:

"You are the salt of the earth. But if the salt loses its saltiness, how can it be made salty again? It is no longer good for anything, except to be thrown out and trampled by men." Mt 5:13

Then, as the sun settled behind the mountains in the west, he turned and pointed toward nearby Safed—the little village set right on the top of the mountain. As its evening lights blinked on—the cooking fires in the yards and the lights from the oil lamps shining through the windows—Jesus said:

"You are the light of the world. A city on a hill cannot be hidden. Neither do people light a lamp and put it under a bowl. Instead they put it on its stand, and it gives light to everyone in the house. In the same way, let your light shine before men, that they may see your good deeds and praise your Father in heaven." Mt 5:14-16

All that seems so basic to us now that we tend to forget it. But we must never let it slide by, for it is foundational to all we believe, to all we are. We are followers of God. We are not of this world. We are salt—causing others to thirst after Jesus. We are light. Let it shine so others may see God in you—and give him glory.

12

Healed

... "Lord, if you are willing, you can make me clean." Jesus
reached out his hand and touched the man. "I am willing," he
said. "Be clean!" ... (Mt 8:2-3)

MUCH AS THE DISEASE OF AIDS is viewed today, the ancient
skin disease of leprosy was viewed as one of the most
horrible diseases known to mankind. In Jesus' day it was
known as "the living death." To have leprosy meant you
were condemned. Hopeless.

When Jesus had finished teaching his disciples on the
Mount of Beatitudes, the Bible says, "He came down from
the mountainside, large crowds followed him. A man with
leprosy came and knelt before him and said, 'Lord, if you are
willing, you can make me clean'" (Mt 8:1-2).

Clean? The leper was talking about two kinds of clean.
The first was physical. Leprosy totally devastates the
human body. Now known as Hansen's Disease, it is
virtually non-existent in the Western Hemisphere—and is
curable. In Jesus' day, however, it was known as the curse of
Satan—the worst thing that could happen to any human
being.

The leper was not only physically unclean, he was

ceremonially unclean. The Levitical law banned lepers from associating with non-lepers as a means to keep the disease from spreading. Being declared ceremonially unclean meant you could not have any fellowship with anyone else—even your family. You could only associate with other lepers.

Banished. Defiled. Declared spiritually dead. The leper was compelled to leave his home and wander the earth in darkness, covering his face, warning anyone who came close with his hoarse cry: "Unclean! Unclean!"

In Jesus' day, the law listed sixty-one different contacts which could defile the proper Jew. Being touched by or touching a leper was second only to touching a dead body. No one might come closer than six feet to a leper, and it was even illegal to speak to a leper, or for him to speak to you. He was hated by others and believed himself hated by God. Such a man came to Jesus.

Jesus did not hesitate. He did something no other man would dare do. He reached out and touched the leper, laying his hand on that horrible body of oozing welts and tumors.

That a man would love enough to touch a leper was unbelievable. Jesus, however, was God—and God is love. It is God's nature to touch the unlovely, the untouchable. Jesus, therefore, did the unthinkable. He touched the leper. When he did, the man was instantly healed.

It was not only the disease which brought hopelessness— it was man's reaction to the disease. Jesus had but one purpose in life—to help the hopeless. In this case he overrode the law of Moses with the law of love. But he did more: he overrode the law of nature with the law of healing. He was not fearful of demons, infection, or the law. There was only one law—the law of love. The duty of compassion, the obligation of love, took precedence over all other rules and laws and regulations.

A doctor never sees a sick baby as a menace, rather he sees the infant as a hurting child needing to be healed. No loving daddy, seeing his helpless child under attack, hesitates to rush to save the child. The law of love rules in such situations. The true child of God will break any convention and will take any risk to help someone in need—even if that person had been declared untouchable by others.

We are surrounded by frightened people the world calls unclean: homosexuals, child molesters, drug addicts, the victims of AIDS. Maybe you know one of them. What a wonderful opportunity to go to them—in prisons and hospitals—and in the name of Jesus to carry the good news that healing is available—even be the hand of Jesus as you reach out and touch them.

13

Authority over Evil Spirits

... *"What is this? ... He even gives orders to evil spirits and they obey him."* (Mk 1:27)

JESUS BEGAN HIS PUBLIC MINISTRY on the shores of the Sea of Galilee. "The time has come," he said. "The kingdom of God is near. Repent and believe the good news."

Near where I am today, sitting on an old stone wall in the ruins of old Capernaum on the northern shore, Jesus called his first disciples. "As Jesus was walking beside the Sea of Galilee, he saw two brothers, Simon, called Peter and his brother Andrew. They were casting a net into the lake, for they were fishermen. 'Come, follow me,' Jesus said, 'and I will make you fishers of men.' At once they left their nets and followed him" (Mt 4:18-20).

Galilee! You can't say the name without thinking peace. Yet the region, while appearing to be peaceful on the surface, was a war zone of demonic activity. In fact, it seems every place Jesus traveled in the early days of his ministry, moving from one small town around the shore of this lake to another, he encountered demons.

His first ministry was in the little towns surrounding this

beautiful inland lake. In Capernaum he taught in the synagogue. His teaching gave the people a new awareness of the kingdom of God. For the first time they began to understand that God was not a policeman, a bully, a stern judge. He is a loving Heavenly Father who has a plan and purpose for each life.

But Jesus' teaching, his miracles, his presence also stirred up the demons who operate in the unseen world. Whenever Jesus came into a place where the demons lived, whenever he approached a man or woman where demons had taken residence, it had the same effect as a man poking a stick into a hornet's nest. The demons went crazy.

That happened in the synagogue in Capernaum. It was a Saturday morning and Jesus was there to teach. Here's the way Mark tells the story. "The people were amazed at his teaching, because he taught them as one who had authority, not as the teachers of the law. Just then a man in their synagogue who was possessed by an evil spirit cried out, 'What do you want with us, Jesus of Nazareth? Have you come to destroy us? I know who you are—the Holy One of God!' " (Mk 1:22-24).

Although the people on earth were slow to recognize Jesus as the Son of God, the demons recognized him instantly. They knew him from heaven, where they had lived with their leader, Lucifer, before they were all cast out following what Isaiah calls a "war in heaven."

When Jesus appeared in their midst on earth, the demons were anguished and often caused the men and women in whom they were living to act violently—just as they still do. In this case, Jesus ordered the evil spirit to come out of the man. The man began to shake violently and screech—but was instantly delivered. The people in the synagogue were amazed: "What's this? He even gives orders to evil spirits and they obey Him."

Throughout his ministry on earth, Jesus took authority

over demons. Just a few days before he ascended into heaven, Jesus told his disciples he was going to give them the same power over demons that he had. "But you will receive power when the Holy Spirit comes on you" (Acts 1:8).

What hope. We are not subject to evil spirits. They are subject to us.

14

Power

... "Everything is possible for him who believes." (Mk 9:23)

IT WAS A BEAUTIFUL AUTUMN DAY when Jesus and his disciples gathered near the base of snow-capped Mt. Hermon. At 9,101 feet Mt. Hermon is the highest mountain in the Middle East. From its snow-capped summit flow the headwaters of the Jordan River, the source for both the Sea of Galilee and the Dead Sea—far to the south.

A series of significant events took place on these slopes, beginning when Jesus commissioned the twelve men who had become his disciples. Luke recounts that incident saying, "He gave them power and authority to drive out all demons and to cure diseases, and he sent them out to preach the kingdom of God and to heal the sick" (Lk 9:1-2). They returned with stories of marvelous success.

Then, a week later, Jesus took Peter, James, and John, and climbed the mountain to a place near the timberline. I was up there yesterday, walking all the way to the edge of the snow cap. It's hard to imagine Jesus climbing that far, for the terrain is rugged and I was out of breath with cramping legs. What a robust, physical man he must have been. Once I got there and rested on a moss-covered rock in the quietness, I began to feel the powerful presence of God. I finally had to slip to my knees in worship. Like so many places off the beaten track in Israel, this is a sacred spot.

The three men remained with Jesus on the mountainside for three days—fasting and praying. On the second day, an incredible thing happened. Jesus' face radically changed. His clothes became as bright as lightning. As his disciples watched, awestruck, two other men appeared and talked to Jesus. His disciples recognized them as Moses and Elijah. Moses had been dead more than 1,000 years. Elijah had died 600 years before. Yet here they were, talking to Jesus. What wonderful proof that we live on after death!

Scared speechless, the men watched until the apparitions disappeared and Jesus resumed his normal appearance. Only then did Peter stammer, "This is wonderful. Let's build a monument. In fact, let's build three of them—and just stay here where the glory is."

"Not here. Not on this mountain." Jesus said. "There's work to do in the valley, and the time is short." So, picking up their things they descended to a place very near where I'm standing today. And suddenly they were caught up in a great human drama, facing what seemed to be an impossible situation.

How typical of us all. One moment we are with God on a mountaintop. The next we're caught up in the swirl of human need. Faced with problems that rip at our heart and send us to the brink of despair.

The rest of his disciples had gotten embroiled in an argument with the religious Jews about demons. Can a godly man be possessed of demons? If he is afflicted with demons, is he oppressed, obsessed, or possessed? What methods should you use to exorcise demons? Can a child be possessed by demons?

Jesus never got involved in these arguments. He just cast the demons out and went on his way.

This time it must have been especially exasperating to

Jesus. He must have wanted to be alone in this beautiful place, quietly talking to God. He had only a short time to live. He would be tortured and executed as a criminal. He really needed to be quiet and assimilate all he had just experienced on the Mount of Transfiguration. Instead, Jesus was thrust into the middle of a silly argument and realized the men he'd been training to take over when he left were powerless.

But Jesus never turned away from human need. "What's the argument about?" he asked.

A man stepped forward. "Teacher, I brought you my son, who is possessed by a spirit that has robbed him of speech. Whenever it seizes him, it throws him to the ground. He foams at the mouth, gnashes his teeth and becomes rigid. I asked your disciples to drive out the spirit, but they could not" (Mk 9:17-18).

A sad spectacle. Like many Christians of today, the disciples had held out great hopes, they had talked of power and authority, but when it came down to being able to do anything—they were helpless.

The boy's father, however, was not discouraged. He seemed to know, in the deep place of his heart, that despite the failures of God's people, despite the seeming powerlessness of the church, despite the public failures of many of God's servants, despite the big-tell, no-show of the professional religionist—if he could just get to Jesus, his son would be healed. That's the source, the only source, of spiritual power.

Jesus recognized the genuineness of the father's faith. Turning to the child, he spoke to the evil spirit: "You deaf and dumb spirit, I command you, come out of him and never enter him again." The demon threw the child to the ground, then in a horrible screech—left. The child was free.

Jesus didn't come just to get us to heaven when we die. He came to give us abundant life here on earth. Free from the bondage of sickness, addictions, and demon possession.

Just because we are Christians, do not think we're immune to attacks from evil spirits. Is there some dark spirit torturing you, driving you, controlling you? If so, Let Jesus cast it out so you can be totally free.

15

Born Again

... "No man can see the kingdom of God unless he is born
again." (Jn 3:3)

E VERY TIME I SEE ONE OF MY adult daughters driving an
automobile I think how marvelous it is that a petite
young woman can climb into such a big piece of machinery
and control its actions. Yet a car is virtually useless, except as
a small shelter from the rain, unless the ignition is turned on.

When I taught my girls how to drive I started with the
ignition. I showed them how to insert the key, turn it, and
start the engine. It was fun, cranking the engine and hearing
it run, knowing you had the power to turn it on and shut it
off. However, once having taught them that, I went on to
other things; for there is far more to driving than turning on
the engine.

Does that mean the ignition is not important since I only
mentioned it once or twice? Absolutely not. It is of *primary*
importance. But to dwell on the ignition means you'll never
learn how to shift gears, much less parallel park or drive on
the freeway in heavy traffic.

All that came to mind last night as I was walking through
the darkened streets of Jerusalem on my way back to my

hotel from where I had been shopping on Ben Yehuda Street. Jesus had used a term that has become synonymous with evangelical Christianity.

Yet, to our knowledge, he used the term only once: that night in Jerusalem when he had his well known conversation with Nicodemus. "You must be born again," he told him (Jn 3:7).

Since Jesus said it only once, does that mean that new birth is relatively unimportant? Absolutely not. Being born again is as important to our entering the kingdom of God as turning the ignition is to driving a car, or as the birth experience is to life itself.

The new birth is the starting place of the Christian life. Everything else depends on it. The person who is attending church but hasn't been born again is like a person sitting in a car, twisting the wheel, putting on the turn signals, honking his horn—but going nowhere because he or she has never turned on the ignition.

Nicodemus was a Pharisee—a religious Jew. Not only that, he was a member of the Jewish ruling council in Jerusalem, a highly select group of 72 men called the Sanhedrin. Even so, his heart was hungry for spiritual truth. It was not enough to keep all the laws. Nicodemus wanted a relationship with God. He was not satisfied with sitting in his stalled car and blowing the horn. He was not satisfied with playing religious games. He wanted to go all the way with God.

But Nicodemus was fearful—fearful of what the other members of the Sanhedrin would say if they saw him with Jesus. So he sought Jesus out at night, and opened his heart to him with honest questions. "Rabbi, we know you are a teacher who has come from God. For no one could perform the miraculous signs you are doing if God were not with him" (Jn 3:2).

Jesus didn't even thank him for recognizing him. He just bore into the heart of the matter. "Nicodemus, unless a man is born again he cannot see the kingdom of God."

Nicodemus wanted to argue logic. How can a grown man be born again? But Jesus was not talking about physical birth. He was speaking of spiritual birth. To enter the kingdom of God you must repent of your sinful nature, die to self, and be born again. It is the most important decision any man or woman or child will ever make. And it must be made. The choice is ours. That decision is made by an act of the will. Until we make it, we have not entered the kingdom of God.

Jesus closed that conversation by telling Nicodemus it's not hard to be born again. All you are doing is responding to God's love. "For God so loved the world," Jesus told him, "that he gave his one and only Son—that whoever believes in him shall not perish but have eternal life. For God did not send his Son into the world to condemn the world, but to save the world through him. Whoever believes in him is not condemned, but whoever does not believe stands condemned already because he has not believed in the name of God's one and only Son" (Jn 3:16-18).

It's one of the big themes of the Bible: decision. The American poet, James Russell Lowell, seized on that theme in *This Present Crisis*.

Once to every man and nation comes the moment
    to decide;
In the strife of Truth with Falsehood,
    for the good or evil side;
Some great cause, God's new Messiah,
    offering each the bloom or blight,
Parts the goats upon the left hand and sheep
    upon the right,
And the choice goes by forever twixt that darkness
    and that light.

When life is over, nothing else matters but that I know him and those most precious to me know him also.

16

What Is Prayer?

After leaving them, he went up on a mountain to pray. (Mk 6:46)

I'M SITTING ON THE EDGE OF A 1000-foot cliff at the top of Mt. Arbel, overlooking the Sea of Galilee. Below me and to my right is the modern city of Tiberias. To my left, at the north end of this beautiful, natural lake, are the ruins of the ancient city of Capernaum—where Jesus lived the last three years of his life on earth. Just beyond the low mountains behind me is Nazareth, the village of his childhood.

Jesus often came up on this mountain to pray. It was then, as it is today, a quiet spot. Despite its beauty, few people come here because of the difficulty of the climb.

Just over this ledge and about halfway down the cliff are the ancient cliff-dwellings of the Zealots—Jewish rebels who conducted guerrilla warfare against the Romans in the days of Jesus. One of his disciples, Simon the Zealot, belonged to this group.

The Bible says Jesus often withdrew to pray. He was constantly aware of the warfare raging in the invisible world around us. Jesus knew that prayer was the only way to win that war.

The devil is still here. His demons are all around us. We

can't see them, but they're here just the same.

In his letter to the Ephesians Paul tells Christians to make certain they dress in the full armor of God so that when the enemy attacks, they'll be protected. But we have to do more than dress daily in the armor of God. Most important, Paul says, we are to "pray in the Spirit on all occasions with all kinds of prayers and requests" (Eph 6:18). Jesus did that when he came to this mountain to pray.

One time, Mark writes, "Very early in the morning, while it was still dark, Jesus got up, left the house and went off to a solitary place, where he prayed" (Mk 1:35).

Luke talks about the huge crowds which followed Jesus. "But Jesus," Luke says, "often withdrew to lonely places and prayed" (Lk 5:16).

"One of those days," Luke writes, "Jesus went out to a mountainside to pray, and spent the night praying to God" (Lk 6:12).

Two things seemed especially important to Jesus: solitude and prayer.

What is prayer? Here is a simple, two-part definition: prayer is talking to God; prayer is God talking to you.

Today's Jews often go to the Western Wall in Jerusalem where they stick written prayers into the cracks. That is a form of prayer—but only half of it. For prayer is more than speaking—or writing—to God. Prayer is also hearing from God.

Prayer is not a posture you take, as a yogi might do. Nor is it a formula, repeating certain words—even Scripture. Prayer does not depend on whether you're good or bad, a Christian, Jew, or a heathen. Prayer is a two-way conversation with God. The creature talking with his Creator—and God talking back.

In the middle of his teaching in the Sermon on the Mount, Jesus paused, looked at his disciples, and realized they knew virtually nothing about prayer. They knew how to *say* prayers, just as they knew how to wrap themselves in a prayer shawl. But they were ignorant when it came to having a conversation with God.

So Jesus warned them against "babbling like pagans." He told them, instead of praying long public prayers, to go into their room, close the door, and talk to God as a child talks to his father. These words remain the best counsel for those of us who really want to know God.

17

Touching the World

"Whoever believes in me, as the Scripture has said, streams of living water will flow from within him." (Jn 7:38)

WITH THE EXCEPTION OF HIS TRIP INTO EGYPT when he was an infant, Jesus never traveled more than 100 miles from his hometown. That's hard to believe in today's world. Here I am in Israel, 10,000 miles from home. I think nothing of getting on a plane in Florida and flying to California—or Singapore. Each morning my oldest son gets in his car and drives farther to and from work at the Kennedy Space Center than Jesus ever traveled in his lifetime. And think about those people who climb aboard one of the space shuttles and take off for outer space. Incredible.

Yet that man, who never went anywhere, preached a message that has gone everywhere—and has radically changed the entire world more than anything anyone else has ever said or done.

Yesterday we were in southern Israel near Jericho at the Dead Sea, which was as far south as Jesus ever traveled from his home in Capernaum.

Today I'm in northern Israel close to the Lebanese border. It took me less than one day by car to cover the entire length of this nation. And this afternoon, when we leave here, we'll cover the width of the nation in less than two hours. It is, indeed, a small country.

A few minutes ago I waded in a small, fast moving stream which is one of the headwater streams of the Jordan River. There are three major streams in northern Israel which form the upper Jordan. The water comes from springs and the melting snow from Mt. Hermon. Flowing south it empties into the Sea of Galilee, 600 feet below sea level. The water then flows on from its southern exit in Galilee through the Jordan Valley and eventually empties into the Dead Sea— 1300 feet below sea level.

Do you believe that a snowflake on Mt. Hermon, mingling with billions of other snowflakes, can become one of the most famous rivers in the world?

Just as a single snowflake may not look like much, so the people of Jesus' day did not regard his ministry as of lasting consequence. In fact, many of the religious leaders actually said he was demon-possessed. Others simply ignored him. Yet Jesus' power continues on today, even as the River Jordan has continued its southern course throughout history.

Jesus crossed the Jordan many times. In winter, when the river is swollen by rains, it is a treacherous crossing which can only be made in certain places. Following the dry season in late fall, the Jordan is often nothing more than a small stream, meandering through the valley on its way to the Dead Sea.

A river, like the Spirit which flowed out of Jesus, touches places of which its source knows nothing. Jesus often referred to this truth when talking to his disciples. He was not concerned that his earthly life would soon be over. He knew he was eternal. Jesus knew that the death of his body would in no way stop him—for he would live forever. On several occasions he reminded his followers that if they believed in him, they would live forever also. Speaking of the continuing power of his Spirit in them—and in us—he said, "Whoever believes in me, as the Scripture has said, streams of living water will flow from within him" (Jn 7:38).

In other words, if we have received his Spirit, no matter how small and insignificant we may think our lives are, out of us will flow rivers that will bless the uttermost parts of the earth. None of this is our responsibility, but the work of the Spirit. All we have to do is believe in God's word. Indeed, God rarely allows a person to see how great a blessing he or she is.

I've followed the Jordan from its headwaters to the place where it empties into the Dead Sea. This is a persistent river which overcomes all barriers. It often changes course depending on the force of its power and the amount of water it is carrying. On many occasions military men or farmers have tried to dam it up and divert its flow. They may succeed temporarily, but the mighty force of the river—even though it seems small when compared to rivers such as the Mississippi, the Nile, or the Amazon—always makes a channel around the obstacle so the water can reach its final destination.

I've seen this happen, over and over, in the lives of God's men and women. We come to an obstacle which seems too great to overcome. We are diverted when the barrier seems too high to get around. But if we pay attention to our source—rather than the barrier—we are always victorious. It is only when we focus on the obstacle, rather than the power of our source, that we are defeated.

Jesus never focused on the obstacles. At one time Satan, instead of building a dam, dug a hole. Jesus merely went underground, and then emerged with more power than ever before.

The river of the Spirit of God overcomes all obstacles. In fact, the barrier is a matter of indifference to the river which is pushed, not by its own power, but by the power of its source.

We need never allow anything to come between us and

Jesus Christ, our source of power. Do not be dismayed by circumstances, sickness, nor the devil's taunts. Keep your eye on Jesus and nothing can deter you from finishing your course.

18

Clouds, God's Curtains

"... They will see the Son of Man coming on the clouds of the sky, with power and great glory." (Mt 24:30)

ISRAEL IS A DRY, BARREN LAND. Most of the nation is desert.

There are exceptions. The lush Jordan Valley is one of them. Irrigated and moistened by the water which flows from the Sea of Galilee to the Dead Sea, here the desert sands produce a variety of foliage and fruit. Northern Israel is the same. The Jezreel Valley is one of the most fertile valleys in the world, producing an abundance of crops.

The region around the Sea of Galilee is also fruitful. Beautiful farms and orchards stretch as far as the eye can see. When the winter rains are over and spring comes in the Galilee, there is no more beautiful spot on earth.

But Israel is a land of contrasts. Travel only a few miles south from the beautiful Galilee and you enter the desolate Judean wilderness where I am today. Beyond that stretches the Negev Desert going south to where it joins the Sinai Peninsula, known in Bible times as "that great and terrible wilderness."

This is wild, desolate territory. Jesus had his encounter with Satan near where I am. He had to go through here on his walks to Jerusalem—sometimes in heat that reached 120 degrees. This was the scene of the most famous of his parables, the story of the Good Samaritan who "went down from Jerusalem to Jericho."

Rain seldom falls here. In fact, the average rainfall is less than three inches a year. The problem is it may not rain for two years—then rain all six inches at one time. When that happens, horrible flooding takes place. The deep canyons, known as wadis, fill up with rampaging, dirty water which has run off the alkaline hills and is rushing downstream toward the Dead Sea. When that happens, anything in the way of the water is swept before it. A number of people have drowned because of these instant desert floods.

Yet rain is always considered a sign of God's blessing in Israel. Especially are clouds welcome here in the wilderness. When King Ahab sinned, God withheld rain for three years. The sign of God's blessing was the appearance of a cloud—the size of a man's hand—which brought with it refreshing and life-giving showers.

Like other natural elements, clouds often appear in the figurative language of the Bible. "A king's favor," Proverbs says, is "like a rain cloud in spring."

The psalmist says God's love and mercy are "higher than the clouds."

Isaiah said, "God has swept away our offenses like a cloud, our sins like the morning mist."

Jude says false teachers are "useless clouds without rain," and Hebrews talks about a "cloud of witnesses," a common classical expression suggesting a crowd gathered for a theater or sporting event.

But clouds are also closely connected with those times when God reveals himself.

When God gave the law to Moses, the top of Mt. Sinai was covered with clouds—accompanied by lightning and thunder.

A bright cloud and fiery pillar led the children of Israel through the wilderness. Day and night the brightly shining cloud stood over the tabernacle in the center of Israel's camp—evidence of God's presence.

As Jesus approached the time of his death he began talking to his disciples about what they should expect in the days and years following. He warned them of wars and rumors of wars, famines and earthquakes, the increase of wickedness in the world. But Jesus also gave them a wonderful message of hope when he said he would return "coming on the clouds of the sky, with power and great glory." What a powerful message that we can all hold on to in these critical days.

The morning Jesus was crucified, a huge cloud appeared over Israel. Matthew, Mark, and Luke all use the same wording. "It was now about the sixth hour and darkness came over the whole land until the ninth hour. From noon until three a cloud covered the entire nation. God himself was in mourning and showed it by covering the sun with the presence of his cloud."

Perhaps the most significant cloud in history was the one that received Jesus when he ascended after his resurrection from the dead. But more significant to us is that the Bible says Jesus will return one day. When he does, it will be in a cloud—the same way he ascended. Keep your eyes on Jesus who is alive in your heart and will one day return to "gather his elect" to himself.

19

The Shepherd

"I am the good shepherd. The good shepherd lays down his life for the sheep." (Jn 10:11)

THROUGHOUT ISRAEL, from the mountainsides around Galilee to deep in the Negev Desert, you find shepherds with their sheep. The same was true when Jesus was here on earth.

Unlike other regions of the world where shepherds are men, most of the shepherds in Israel today are women—and boys and girls. Occasionally you will find a man with a flock of sheep, but among the Bedouins, the wandering nomads who live in the Negev Desert, responsibility for the sheep rests upon the women and children. The men spend much of the day in their tents, drinking tea and handling tribal business.

In the days of Jesus, Israel was primarily agricultural. That has since changed. Big cities have replaced many of the small villages. Tourism has become the nation's number one source of revenue.

However, in the remote regions, and in the northern area of the nation, you still find flocks of sheep—often mixed with goats—following their shepherd across the hillsides.

Jesus likened his ministry to that of the shepherd. He

called himself the Good Shepherd. "I am the good shepherd; I know my sheep and my sheep know me," he said.

Yesterday I sat in a field near a watering trough. Beside it was an open well with a rope attached to a bucket. While I was there three shepherds approached from different directions, all followed by thirsty flocks of sheep. The animals mixed together drinking from the same trough. But when one shepherd was ready to go, all he had to do was whistle. His sheep immediately responded, pulling away from the other sheep and following their shepherd. The sheep knew the shepherd's voice.

After he was resurrected, but before he ascended to heaven, Jesus met one last time with his disciples on the shore of Galilee. Pulling Peter aside he said to him, "Feed my sheep. Feed my lambs." That was important to Jesus—that we take care of his flock.

"My sheep listen to my voice; I know them, and they follow me," Jesus said earlier. "I am the good shepherd," he told his disciples. "The good shepherd lays down his life for the sheep." He was preparing them for what lay ahead when he would die for the sins of the world—a world God so loved that he sent his only Son.

God still calls on us to lay down our lives for the sheep. The night before he was crucified Jesus said: "Greater love has no one than this, that one lay down his life for his friends." That is done in many ways.

Midway through one of the most successful literary careers in history, Elizabeth Barrett, heir to one of the world's largest fortunes, fell in love with Robert Browning— a poor, struggling poet. Her father, who had huge land holdings in Jamaica as well as large estates in England, disapproved of the marriage. He told her if she married Browning he would cut her off from the family's great fortune. Elizabeth, frail and in failing health, made a decision to follow her heart. Rather than live in luxury and write poems for the rich, she would live with her husband and minister to the poor. She wrote:

> I was too ambitious in my deed,
> And thought to distance all men in success,
> Till God came on me, marked the place, and said,
> "Ill-doer, henceforth keep within this line,
> Attempting less than others"—and I stand
> And work among Christ's little ones, content.

Elizabeth Barrett Browning chose the way of the cross. Success, to her, was giving herself to the lambs of Jesus' flock, feeding the sheep.

20

The Watchtower

... *"Day after day ... I stand on the watchtower...."* (Is 21:8)

THE WATCHTOWER WAS A FAMILIAR sight in Jesus' day. Built of the stones taken from a field, it usually sat in the middle of a field or a vineyard. The owner of the field would stand in the watchtower to oversee the workers. From his vantage point during harvest time he could see if anyone was loafing. At night the watchmen would take turns during various "watches" of the night to guard the field—protecting it from foxes, bears, and poachers.

In Old Testament days these towers were used by military watchmen. The soldiers would be looking out for the Philistines, fierce bands of renegades who would wait until the crops were ripe, then swoop down to harvest what other men had cultivated.

Jesus' favorite title for himself was "Son of Man." It was a term used often by the Old Testament prophet Ezekiel. Although Jesus' enemies didn't seem to realize it, the term "Son of Man" referred to the coming Messiah. In one place God told Ezekiel: "Son of man, I have made you a watchman for the house of Israel; so hear the word I speak and give them warning from me."

Jesus saw himself as a watchman—one who came from

God to warn and protect. But he also saw himself as
"husbandman": the ancient term for one who managed, one
who was in charge, an overseer.

Shortly before Jesus was crucified he sat down with his
disciples and told them the story of a husbandman, or
manager, who planted a vineyard. "He put a wall around it,
dug a pit for the winepress and built a watchtower. Then he
rented the vineyard to some farmers and went away on a
journey. At harvest time he sent a servant to the tenants to
collect from them some of the fruit of the vineyard" (Mk
12:1-2).

In Jesus' parable the tenant, the one who was sitting in the
watchtower until the owner returned, beat the three messengers who came from the owner, killing one of them. The
owner then sent additional servants to collect what was due
him, and the tenant manager treated them the same way.
Finally the owner sent his son. "Surely they will respect
him," the owner said. But the tenant managers saw this as
an opportunity to take over completely. They grabbed the
son, threw him out of the vineyard and killed him.

Turning to his disciples, Jesus asked, "What do you think
the owner will do to those tenants when he comes back?"

"There's no doubt what he'll do," they replied. "He'll
bring those villains to a wretched end. Then he will rent the
vineyard to other tenants, who will give him his share of the
crop at harvest time."

Then Jesus did what he often did when he told a parable.
He drew it to a close by quoting from the Old Testament—a
passage that Jesus applied to himself. This time he quoted
from Psalm 118. "The stone the builders rejected has become
the capstone; the Lord has done this and it is marvelous in
our eyes."

Jesus finished his parable with a prophetic explanation.
"The kingdom of God," he said to the Jews, "will be taken
away from you and given to a people who will produce its
fruit." That fascinating prophecy came to pass when the

apostle Paul took the gospel to the gentile world.

The responsibility of being good managers of God's vineyard has now passed to us. Each of us has a sacred obligation, to take care of the field where we are placed, to protect it from the enemy, to see the harvest is taken, and to give back to the owner his rightful share.

You may not think your little field is very important. But God has set you in your field as a watchman. Each one of us has a sphere of influence. Most of us don't realize it, but our influence is much larger than we can ever imagine—and will continue on for generations to come, be it good or evil. It's a wonderful responsibility—frightening at times—but wonderful. Always remember, though, you're never in your watchtower alone. Jesus is ever with you, and his Spirit will whisper just the things you need to say and do.

Keep watch over your field, your vineyard: your family, your church, your health, your money, your faith—all the things you are responsible for. You are the tenant manager. But never forget who owns the field.

21

Even the Wind and
the Waves Obey Him

. . . "Who is this? Even the wind and the waves obey him!"

(Mk 4:41)

THE SEA OF GALILEE is one of the most beautiful places on earth. The very name evokes all kinds of memories. Not far from where I sit today, listening to the gentle waves lapping against the rocky shore, Jesus called his disciples and told them to lay aside their nets—that he would make them fishers of men. Some place out there Jesus walked on the water. Another time, standing on the eastern shore, he called to his disciples who were fishing and told them to lower their nets on the other side of the boat. They did, and their catch was so great they could barely pull in all the fish.

But the story that sticks in everyone's mind is the story of the dark and stormy night when Jesus and his disciples were crossing the lake from Capernaum to the southern shore. It's hard to imagine, since the water is so smooth and peaceful this morning. But this lake can, in an instant, become a death trap.

The lake is surrounded on three sides by high mountains. At 660 feet below sea level, it is in the middle of a natural funnel. When the wind blows off the surrounding mountains it means instant waves—huge ones.

It was after sundown when Jesus finished teaching near Capernaum. He then got into an open fishing boat owned by his disciples and asked them to take him to the far end of the lake—a distance of about 13 miles.

They were tough seamen, these disciples. But that night, when a furious squall came up, and the towering waves broke over the boat so it was nearly swamped, the disciples were afraid. This was no ordinary storm. Satan himself was trying to drown them.

Oblivious to the storm, Jesus was asleep in the stern— curled up on the fishing nets. The disciples couldn't believe he could sleep through such a storm.

"Master, don't you care if we drown?"

Stretching himself, Jesus looked around at the storm, then stood up and took authority over the waves. Incredible. He literally spoke—or shouted it seems—at the elements. He spoke as a drill-sergeant speaks to a bunch of recruits. "Shut up," Jesus barked at the wind. Then turning to the waves he commanded, "Sit down."

These were the identical words he had used the week before when he spoke to a demon which was trying to kill a man in Capernaum. Jesus had been teaching in the synagogue when the demon interrupted the service, causing the man to begin screaming. Jesus looked at the man—but spoke to the demon. He commanded it to first "Shut up!" Then he commanded it to come out of the man. It did.

I've learned you don't speak to demons gently, any more than you would be gentle with a striking rattlesnake. You act with authority—and, if necessary, force.

What Jesus did that night when he calmed the storm was to take authority. He did it not to save his life and the lives of the others in the boat, for he had already spoken and said they were going over to the other side. Once Jesus says a thing is going to happen, it does. No, he took action to show his disciples that they, too, had authority over anything that tried to thwart God's will. That's why, after it was over, he chided the men on their "little faith."

Jesus came to earth to restore humanity to our rightful place of dominion over all things—evil, sickness, anything that would keep us from doing what God wants. Dominion means being in charge of this world. Adam had dominion in the Garden of Eden, but he lost it when he sinned. He forgot his authority came from God. Once people begin to act as if they own this world, as if they are their own boss, that they can do anything they want—then they are no longer qualified to receive God's authority. God's authority is given only to those who submit their lives to God.

Satan cannot stop what God has ordained. Jesus came to remind us that his authority is ours as well. We can take dominion over the storms battering our lives, and the lives of our families. Take the authority God has given you in Jesus. Say to those storms: "In the name of Jesus, shut up! Sit down!" Then get on about your life with peace and joy.

22

Letting Faith Turn a Little into a Lot

"Here is a boy with five small barley loaves and two small fish, but how far will they go among so many?" (Jn 6:9)

ONE OF THE MOST THRILLING EXPERIENCES in life was my first glimpse of the Sea of Galilee. This afternoon as we approached Galilee from Nazareth with the sun behind us, I found myself almost unable to breathe, so great was the sense of God's presence in this place.

Every time I see it the Bible stories come rushing through my mind like a spring brook racing over the rocks in a creek bed. It was in the villages around this lake, and in the surrounding hills, that Jesus spent most of his time, where he taught and ministered. In these beautiful hills he found people in great need—and touched them with his healing hands. Lepers, dying children, the blind and deaf, the crippled and broken—Jesus healed them all.

There is an awesome sense of beauty and peace here that defies logic, especially in these troubled times.

This afternoon, after wandering through the ruins of old Capernaum, I came down here to the beach on the northern shore of the Galilee. The sun is now setting in the west. Mt.

Arbel, which towers over Tiberias on the western shore, is casting a long shadow out over the deep blue, mirror-like surface of the water. To the east the sun is now lighting the Golan Heights, turning the cliffs and mountains a brilliant gold. Far to the south, extending from the southern edge of the sea and running through the nation of Jordan along the Jordan Valley, are the hills of Moab. They, too, are picking up the last rays of the sun. It is a place of peace and beauty. A quiet place.

But it wasn't quiet that evening when Jesus came here in the spring of the year before he was crucified. The week before Passover brought thousands of pilgrims from the north moving through this area toward Jerusalem. They thronged around Jesus listening to his teaching, amazed as he laid hands on the sick and they were instantly healed.

This was a critical time in Jesus' life. Word had just come that Herod had executed John the Baptist. Jesus expected the people to react against John's execution, which would bring swift reprisals from the Roman overlords. The Romans would probably blame him as one of the insurrectionists. It would be wise to withdraw until the clamor died down.

Jesus got into a small boat and his disciples rowed him around the lake from Capernaum to where a gentle field slopes down to the water. It was near where he had taught his disciples the Sermon on the Mount. But the huge mob of people, numbering more than 5,000 men plus their families, rushed along the shoreline, following his boat until he pulled ashore.

It must have been frustrating—seldom finding time to be alone. Yet the people were hungry for God. John wrote that Jesus had "compassion" on them. As evening fell Jesus turned to Philip and said with a twinkle in his eye, "It looks like we're going to have to feed this bunch."

Philip must have turned pale. Philip, like Andrew and Peter, was from nearby Bethsaida. Since they were near their hometown, Philip thought Jesus meant for him to go into town and buy food.

"We can't afford to feed 5,000 people," he blurted out.

Andrew, who had overheard Jesus' question to Philip, stepped forward. He had a small boy in tow. The boy had his picnic lunch with him—five barley loaves and two small, sardine-sized fish. "Will this help?" the boy asked. It was all Jesus needed.

While Philip had no faith at all, Andrew—and the little boy—were at least willing to try. Their faith illustrates a basic spiritual principle. If you will just work with what you have, offering to God what little bit you have, God will do the multiplication.

Taking the bread, Jesus blessed it with an ancient Jewish grace over meals. "Blessed art thou, Jehovah our God, King of the universe, who causes bread to come forth from the earth."

"Take it and distribute it," Jesus told his disciples. Nobody really knows when the miracle took place. In the blessing? In the distribution? In the eating? But suddenly there was enough food to feed all 5,000 people. When the people had eaten their fill the twelve disciples passed among them with their *kophinos*—large wicker baskets which they slung from their shoulders. The people filled the baskets with leftovers.

No one knows what happened to the leftovers. Maybe Jesus offered some to the little boy to take home. Maybe he told his disciples to distribute them among the poor of the nearby cities. Maybe he let his disciples keep them, since they had to eat, too. No one knows. The lesson of the story, however, is not the leftovers. It's the miracle of a little boy who gave everything he had—and how God used it to bless a multitude. Are we willing to give to God what little we have—trusting him to use it to bless us and others?

23

Christ or Caesar

"They overcame him by the blood of the Lamb and by the word of their testimony. . . ." (Rv 12:11)

IT'S IMPOSSIBLE TO THINK OF JESUS' ministry here in Israel without being reminded of the powerful impact he made on his followers after he was gone. Many leaders are honored—some even worshiped—while they are here. After they're gone, however, most are soon forgotten.

Wandering around the ruins of the ancient city of Caesarea by the Sea, located midway between Tel Aviv and Haifa on the Mediterranean coast, you find evidence of the powerful influence of Christianity. I'm sitting on an ancient Roman pillar that is lying on its side next to an excavated street called the "Street of Statues." Here the so-called shakers and movers of Roman society were memorialized in stone. For centuries this street, with its long forgotten marble people lining the marble pavement, lay buried in the rubble of forgotten civilizations. Today these chipped, marble statues decorate an open air museum in the city of Caesarea.

No one remembers their names, or what they did.

Not so with Jesus, who received little honor while on earth—eventually being executed as a common criminal.

Perhaps his death was ordered by one of these nameless and forgotten Romans. Yet, Jesus' influence is greater today than ever before.

Caesarea was one of the most glittering cities of the ancient world. Herod the Great spent twelve years and the equivalent of a billion dollars building it. He dedicated it to Caesar Augustus in 10 B.C. It later became the capital of the Roman government in Judea.

This magnificent city was built with blocks of granite floated down the Nile from Aswan, Egypt, and marble brought from Italy. The harbor provided anchorage for as many as 100 Roman war galleys.

South of town are the ruins of the Roman amphitheatre which matched those in Rome and Athens. In the days following the ascension of Jesus, this became a place of horror and death as thousands of Jews accepted Jesus as the Messiah. Christians were lashed to poles in the center of the coliseum and eaten alive by wild animals. Women were crucified on crosses which stood around the perimeter— their murdered babies hung around their necks. Jews were also martyred, especially in A.D. 70 when the Romans held games here to celebrate the destruction of Jerusalem.

Why all this torture and killing? The Romans would not tolerate worship other than to Caesar—their god. Christians knew they could not worship both Jehovah and Caesar. They chose to die rather than renounce Jesus.

Before being thrown to the lions, those early Christians were given a last chance to recant. Some did, and bowing before the statue of Caesar they said in Greek: *"Caesarus este kurios"*—Caesar is Lord. However, the vast majority, having been transformed by the power of the living Christ, refused to deny him. They went to their death singing: *"Christus este kurios"*—Christ is Lord.

Such martyrs are among the ones described in Revelation 12: "They overcame Satan by the blood of the Lamb and by the word of their testimony; they did not love their lives so much as to shrink from death. . . ."

The first statue at the beginning of the ancient Street of Statues is headless. Last night one of the nation's top archaeologists told me the statue was deliberately sculpted without a head.

"The sculpturer knew that the life of the caesar—the king of Rome—was tenuous. The lives of these 'kings forever'—who called themselves immortal—could end at any moment, and a new caesar would be crowned. So rather than have to carve a new statue every time a caesar died or was assassinated, the sculpturer would merely sculpt a new head—and throw away the old one."

Caesars came—and went. Jesus, however, despite his death at the hands of the Romans, lives on—empowering his people with his spirit to spread the kingdom of God to all the world.

The apostle Paul returned from both his second and third missionary trips to the harbor at Caesarea, teeming with Roman war galleys. From here Paul finally sailed for Rome—where he died for his faith. The ministry of Jesus continues, through millions of men like the apostle Paul, even today throughout the world. But the caesars of the world are forgotten, their heads buried under the rubble of hundreds of decayed civilizations.

God doesn't need more caesars. He's simply looking for a few good men and women who will not deny his Son when faced with the lions of this world.

24

The Hem of His Garment

. . . They sent word to all the surrounding country. People brought all their sick to him and begged him to let the sick just touch the edge of his cloak, and all who touched him were healed. (Mt 14:35–36)

HAVE YOU EVER WONDERED what kind of clothes Jesus wore? The New Testament makes it clear that Jesus, like all observant Jews of the first century, wore phylacteries—known as *tefilin*—when he went to pray in the temple or synagogue. These are small leather capsules, held in place by narrow, black leather bands wrapped around the forehead and wrist. They contain tiny slips of parchment inscribed with scriptural passages.

Although Jesus wore tefilin whenever he entered the temple or a synagogue, he was highly critical of Jews who wore them hypocritically. He specifically criticized those who "make their phylacteries wide," showing off their spirituality.

Jesus also wore a prayer shawl, called a *tallit* or *tallith*, and pronounced "TAL-is." In fact, Jesus wore two garments above his undergarments. One was a long tunic, called a *ha-LUK*. It was a light robe, usually made of linen. The one Jesus wore was of unusual design since it was seamless—

woven in one piece of cloth and bunched together at the waist with a belt.

The upper garment, a mantle draped over the tunic, was a heavy shawl usually woven from wool. In Jesus' day it was called a *ta-LIT*.

Unlike the modern Jewish prayer shawl, which is worn only during prayer, the *tallit* was worn whenever a Jewish man went outside. It was these two garments Jesus was referring to in his Sermon on the Mount when he said, "If someone wants to sue you for your robe—your *haluk*—let him have your shawl—your *tallit*—as well."

Today, when you visit synagogues and temples around the world, you still find Orthodox Jews wrapping themselves in their prayer shawls before praying. The shawl is embroidered with 613 tassels around the fringe—one tassel for each of the laws of the Torah, the first five books of the Bible. Thus, when he puts on the prayer shawl, the Jew is actually wrapping himself in the Torah—the law of Moses. It is a beautiful and sacred concept.

In Jesus' day the tallits were an outer garment worn over the tunic. The 613 tassels on the tallit were worn according to Numbers 15:39 to help the wearer "recall all the commandments of the Lord." In Matthew 25 Jesus criticized those who wore long tassels, just as he criticized those who wore elaborate phylacteries to show off their piousness.

One day Jesus was walking along the shore of the Sea of Galilee, talking with his disciples. As often happened, a huge crowd began to throng around him, pushing and shoving. They had heard of his miracles and were eager to see one— or receive one. A woman who had been hemorrhaging for twelve years pushed her way through the crowd, came up behind him and touched the hem of his garment. What she actually touched was one of those sacred tassels hanging from his tallit. Immediately, the Bible says, her bleeding stopped and she felt something happen in her body. The woman knew she had been healed.

Jesus knew the person who had touched the tassel of his shawl had touched with more than her hand—she had touched with her heart. He turned and asked "Who touched me?" The woman fell at his feet, confessing not only that she had touched him, but confessing her illness—which was supposedly "unspeakable" in religious circles.

This was a critical moment in her life. The Levitical law said a woman was ceremonially unclean during her menstrual period. Not only could she not be touched by a man, she could not enter the temple to worship. For twelve years she had not been allowed in the temple or the synagogues, which was the equivalent of being separated from God. Yet, somehow, she had faith that Jesus would not only heal her—he would understand.

Reaching down, Jesus helped her to her feet. Then he spoke, gently, "Daughter, your faith has healed you. Go in peace and be freed from your suffering."

We can still reach out in prayer and touch the hem of Jesus' garment. He is still healing those who touch him with their heart.

25

Life Is a Comedy

"But so that we may not offend them. . . ." (Mt 17:27)

THE WATER IN THE BEAUTIFUL Sea of Galilee is pure enough to drink. It also yields an extraordinary amount of fish.

Perhaps best known is a species known as St. Peter's fish, served in most of the restaurants on the shore of the lake. The male carries the eggs and the young in its mouth. At least once during Jesus' time on earth, the fish carried something else. This delightful, but mystifying story tells of a fish with a coin in its mouth. Simon Peter, who was a commercial fisherman, found the coin, which explains the name of the fish.

Jesus had a free, and often humorous, way of teaching. He loved to laugh and poke fun at people and events. He would have agreed with the American humorist, Garrison Keillor, who once said, "If you believe in the existence of a loving and merciful God, then life is a comedy."

Keillor was not talking about comedy as in jokes. He meant comedy in the Shakespearean sense—as opposed to tragedy. In tragedy, things turn out badly. In comedy, all's well that ends well. Bottom line: If God is really in control, we might as well enjoy life—rather than take it so seriously.

Jesus spent a lot of time walking around the shore of

Galilee. The first disciples were commercial fishermen. Jesus had been trained as a house builder and was perfectly at home among working men, especially these rough, weathered outdoorsmen who rowed heavy boats and fished at night for a living.

Capernaum, on the north shore of the lake, had been home for Jesus since he left Nazareth. He probably stayed with his friend, Simon bar Jonah, the fisherman.

Several decisive events of his life took place in Capernaum. Perhaps because this was home, Jesus felt more free to joke with the people, laugh with them, and poke fun at their stuffy traditions. But always, always with purpose.

That's what Jesus was doing that afternoon when the representative of the high priest, whose job it was to collect the temple tax, arrived in Capernaum from Jerusalem. Every Jew was required to pay a two-drachma temple tax to the high priest in Jerusalem. This was the same high priest who wanted Jesus arrested on charges of treason. Jesus knew this, yet it didn't seem to bother him that much. He didn't take it personally. In fact, he was so relaxed—even knowing that eventually that high priest would have him crucified— that he could joke about the temple tax.

Each year special tax collectors were sent out to collect the annual tax. It was one of these men who arrived that day in Capernaum—looking for Jesus.

Spotting Peter, the tax collector asked, "Does your teacher think he's too good to pay the temple tax?" It was a catch question. The temple representative had been instructed to look for evidence that Jesus believed himself to be the Messiah. If the authorities could prove that, then they could arrest him for blasphemy. But it wasn't time for that yet. Peter assured the tax collector that of course Jesus paid the temple tax. Then he rushed back for Jesus to confirm his statement.

"Well, Peter," Jesus laughed, "what do you think I should

do? Do kings pay taxes, or do they collect taxes from others?"

The question had profound undercurrents. Jesus was saying, "If I am God, then the temple belongs to me—not me to the temple. Actually, the temple should be paying me, not me paying the temple."

"But let's not offend them—at least not yet," Jesus laughed. "But rather than paying the temple tax out of my own pocket—which would be foolish since I own the temple—we'll let my Father pay it. Go down to the lake, bait a hook, and throw out your line. Pull in the first fish that bites. Open its mouth and you'll find, inside, a four-drachma coin—enough for my tax and enough for yours."

The point was clear. God owns and controls all things. Religion is here to serve man, not man to serve religion. What belongs to Caesar, what to God? Give both their due.

26

Building on the Rock

"Therefore everyone who hears these words of mine and puts them into practice is like a wise man who built his house on the rock." (Mt 7:24)

I GOT UP EARLY THIS MORNING, left Jerusalem, and drove part way down the old Roman road toward Jericho. Leaving my car, I took my canteen and hat and have been hiking ever since. I have followed an ancient canyon, or wadi, called Wadi Kelt, which snakes its way deep through the middle of the Judean wilderness all the way to Jericho—15 miles away from where I started. Nothing grows here but a few desert shrubs. It is, indeed, a wilderness.

This area of Israel, where the mountains jut upward from the desert floor, is divided only by these mysterious dried river beds called wadis. Actually, very little rain falls here. But when it does this becomes a wild, terrifying place. These wadis literally fill up with water which runs off the hard, alkaline desert mountains. It races wildly downhill toward the Dead Sea, 1,300 feet below sea level, sweeping everything in its path.

Jesus had this in mind as he closed the Sermon on the Mount. He told a parable about two builders—one wise, the other foolish. We know it as the story of two houses—one built on rock and the other built on sand. Although Jesus was called a carpenter, the word also means builder. While Jesus may have worked with hammer and saw, most of the building in those days was with stone—rather than wood. He was, in all probability, a general contractor. His parable shows a knowledge of the kinds of foundations necessary to build properly.

"Therefore everyone who hears these words of mine and puts them into practice is like a wise man who built his house on the rock. The rain came down, the streams rose, and the winds blew and beat against that house; yet it did not fall, because it had its foundation on the rock. But everyone who hears these words of mine and does not put them into practice is like a foolish man who built his house on sand. The rain came down, the streams rose, and the winds blew and beat against that house, and it fell with a great crash" (Mt 7:24-27).

As I walked along this dry river bed, kicking the sand with my shoes, I could picture Jesus walking this same wadi. Pausing to sit on a rock, he told his little story. But this parable is more than a story of two houses. It's a wonderful story about life.

Life is full of crises. Loved ones die. Great opportunities are lost. Disease strikes. You may lose your job—or your spouse. Crisis reveals true character. When the water rises, you reveal the kind of foundation you have laid.

You have a choice where you will build your life. The lazy man would find it easy to pitch his tent on this soft, inviting sand. It's easy to build here. This wadi stays dry most of the year. It has a beautiful, flat, sandy bottom. There's no land to clear. No foundations to dig. All you need to do is drive your tent pegs into the sand and you have instant shelter. Then pray it doesn't rain.

But the wise man knows it will rain. Maybe not tonight. Or tomorrow. But one day. Or as the old preacher used to say: "Payday, someday."

The wise man knows rain will come, so he builds on the mountainside. He finds a rocky ledge, high above the bottom of the wadi, and builds for the future.

If you were to follow me down this wadi toward Jericho you would come to St. George's monastery, built by Greek monks hundreds of years ago. It is accessible only from the far side of this deep valley. It took many years to fasten the foundation firmly on the solid granite of the steep precipice, but the monks knew the value of building on the rock— high above the easy sands of the wadi floor.

It's tough to build up there on the rocky ledges. You have to drill into the rock to put down your foundations. But come November, and the rainy season, you're glad you did.

So many people live "just for today." They never pause to think of the result of their actions, or what might happen tomorrow. Jesus wants us to build our lives for the long haul, rather than sacrificing ourselves for instant pleasure.

Solid rock living is hearing God and doing what God says in his word—the Bible. Solid rock living is building for the future, with eternity's values in view.

27

The King and His Kingdom

. . ."The kingdom of heaven is near." (Mt 10:7)

T HE NUMBER ONE SUBJECT OF THE GOSPELS is the kingdom of God. In the early days of his public ministry Jesus spent most of his time doing three things: teaching in the synagogues; preaching the good news of the kingdom; and healing every disease and sickness.

The term "kingdom" was always on Jesus' tongue. But he was not talking about a realm—like the United Kingdom of Great Britain. He was talking about a rule, a reign.

On several occasions Jesus came to where I'm sitting this morning near the site of the ancient temple at the western wall in Jerusalem. Today is the traditional day of the week for Jewish boys to receive their bar mitzva at the western wall. The plaza is teeming with people, families, and tribal groups from all over the world. The term "bar mitzva" literally means "son of the covenant." To the Jews it is on this day that a boy becomes a man and inherits the covenant of Abraham. It is a momentous occasion when one of these 13-year-old boys comes out of the underground chamber carrying the elaborate Torah box, surrounded by the men in his family who are singing and dancing.

From an early age Jews are trained to love and respect the law of God. The Jews of Jesus' day believed, as the modern Jews still do, that the kingdom of God was nationalistic. They believed the Messiah would establish a military, political, earthly kingdom as in the time of King David.

But when Jesus spoke of the kingdom, he had something else in mind. He was not establishing an earthly kingdom, but putting his kingdom into the hearts of men. No longer would Satan have dominion over those who have faith in God. Jesus had come to destroy Satan's dominion.

He did this by deliberately challenging Satan on his own ground. Jesus healed the sick and cast out demons. It was spiritual warfare. The battle was being fought over the ownership of human beings—would they belong to God or Satan?

Jesus invaded other areas where Satan had long held dominion.

Hunger: Jesus fed the 5,000 near the Sea of Galilee.

Natural catastrophes: Jesus calmed the storm on the sea.

Sickness: Jesus cured many who had diseases by speaking a word or touching with his hand.

Death: Not only did he raise several from the dead, but on Easter Sunday Jesus overcame death himself.

In all these battles Jesus was, and continues to be, victor.

The Jews didn't understand this. They were so bound in their traditions they could not fathom how a fellow Jew, an ordinary man, could be the Son of God. After all, he wasn't even a priest. So they continued with their prayers, begging God to send the Messiah—not realizing that he was already among them.

Near the end of his life on earth, Jesus told his disciples that the kingdom of God would continue as long as the king reigned in their hearts. "As you go, preach this message: 'The kingdom of heaven is near,' " he told them. In short: the king is here. How were they to show the world the king was here? "Heal the sick, raise the dead, cleanse those who have leprosy, drive out demons. Freely you have received—now freely give."

You have received the Holy Spirit from me, Jesus said, now give him to all you meet.

Jesus reigns over his kingdom. He is champion over all darkness. He is our healer, our savior, our king.

28

Sabbath Rest

"Remember the Sabbath day by keeping it holy." (Ex 20:8)

NOTHING CHARACTERIZES JEWISH LIFE as much as the Sabbath. *Shabbot*, in Hebrew. The Hebrew word, *shabbot*, literally means *rest* and is taken from Genesis 2:2 where on the seventh day of creation God rested. He hallowed that day for all mankind. Later God translated that into the fourth commandment. The Sabbath is still venerated by Jews all over the world as the primary thing that sets them apart from the world.

Here in Israel everything changes on the Sabbath. All Jewish shops close on Friday evening and stay closed until the same time Saturday. The Jewish buses do not run. The elevators in the Jewish hotels go into automated sequence, which means they automatically stop at every floor so the Orthodox do not have to "work" by pushing a button. Electric lights in homes come on and off automatically so Jews do not have to throw switches—which would be work. Even El Al, the national airline, does not take off or land on *Shabbot*. Meals—in hotel kitchens as well as homes—are cooked the day before and kept warm in special warming ovens which work automatically. It is a special day—a day of rest, family recreation, and worship.

The Sabbath begins at sundown on Friday and ends at sundown Saturday. In Jewish homes it is welcomed as the women of the house light the *Shabbot* candles. Then the family sits at table together and the father goes through the ritual of reading from the Torah, praying, leading the family in singing, then blessing the bread and wine before the Sabbath meal. Jesus also kept the Sabbath. It was to him a holy day—a day of delight.

Although the Sabbath was important to Jesus and his followers, many of today's Christians no longer observe it.

I expressed that frustration to a rabbi yesterday. "The Sabbath is not just for Jews," he said. "It is for all people."

There are two versions of the Ten Commandments—one in Exodus and another in Deuteronomy. While Exodus says to *remember* the Sabbath, Deuteronomy says to *observe* or *keep* the Sabbath. In the Jewish *kiddush*, which is recited over a cup of wine to usher in the Sabbath, both these concepts are found. "Thou hast graciously given us Thy holy Sabbath as a heritage in remembrance of creation . . . the first among the holy convocations to recall the exodus from Egypt."

God gave us the Sabbath to remind us that we are people of great worth. The Jews believe the Sabbath is for all people—not just Jews. Therefore it is unthinkable for a Jew to hire someone to work *for* him on the Sabbath—because the person he would hire should be observing the Sabbath also. We keep the Sabbath, not just so the human body can rest, but to bring us into God's presence in a new and fresh way every week. It is to be a time of celebration and joy.

But the Jews of Jesus' day carried these restrictions far beyond what God had intended. In fact, the laws were so restrictive you could hardly breathe. You were forbidden to lace your sandals since that was work. You were forbidden to walk more than a certain number of paces. When Jesus spit on the ground and made mud to put on the eyes of a blind man to heal him, the Pharisees went into a rage and said that he had broken the Sabbath by making mud.

One day in a grain field near the Sea of Galilee, the disciples began to pick some heads of grain. They rubbed them in their hands and ate the kernels. Pharisees saw them and shouted: "What you are doing is unlawful."

Jesus gently reminded them that "The Son of Man is Lord of the Sabbath."

In short, he was saying, "I, God, created the Sabbath for your benefit. I made the rule to start with and I alone am capable of interpreting it."

Keeping and *remembering* the Sabbath are both important. Even more important, however, is man's relationship with the Lord of the Sabbath.

29

I Was Blind But Now I See!

"... One thing I do know. I was blind but now I see!" (Jn 9:25)

THE POOL OF SILOAM is one of the landmarks of Jerusalem. In Jesus' day it was just inside the Water Gate in the old wall around the city.

This gate opened out over the Kidron Valley. There at the foot of the City of David was the Spring Gihon, where the water still flows abundantly, emptying out into the valley and watering the fig and almond trees.

Seven hundred years before Christ the spring had been vital to the city's survival. In the event of a military siege, the spring was completely exposed and could be cut off, leaving the city without water. In the year 701 B.C., King Hezekiah feared an attack by the Assyrian empire. He told his engineers to carve a tunnel through solid rock under the old city wall to carry water from the spring to a pool inside.

That tunnel, which is a quarter of a mile long and emerges into the pool of Siloam, still carries water.

It was to this pool that Jesus sent a man born blind. A debate erupted between his disciples when they spotted a blind man beside the road. "Who sinned that this man was born blind?" Jesus corrected them. They were asking the wrong question. They were focusing on the *cause* of his blindness, rather than the *cure* for his blindness. Jesus tried to effect a cure before dealing with the cause.

Then Jesus did a strange thing. He spit in the dust of the road, stooped over and made a mud ball with his fingers. Then, wiping it on the eyes of the blind man, he told him, "Go, wash in the pool of Siloam."

That act had special meaning for the Jews. It was from the pool of Siloam the priests drew water for ceremonial washing. There was one significant difference, however. When the Jews washed with ceremonial water they remained the same. When this man washed, he received a miracle. The difference was the touch of Jesus. Jesus could have just spoken to the man and said, "Be healed." But in this case he wanted the man to participate in the healing.

Instead of bringing joy to the people around him, the man's healing caused a terrible religious debate. Since the miracle had taken place on the Sabbath, the religious Jews were angered that Jesus had broken the Sabbath law forbidding work. He had labored, they said, in making mud. They called the man in and tried to force him to testify against Jesus. All he could say was, "Whether he is a sinner or not, I don't know. One thing I do know. I was blind, but now I see!"

The Pharisees threw the man out of the synagogue—banished him from fellowship. Confused, he returned to the pool where he had received his sight.

Looking down in the water, he saw the reflection of another face behind him—a face so kind, so wonderful all he could do was gasp. The second man spoke, and he recognized the voice. It was the voice of the miracle-worker.

"Do you believe in the Son of Man—the Messiah?"

"Who is he, sir?" the man asked. "Tell me so that I may believe in him."

Jesus said, "You have now seen him." In that instant the eyes of the man's heart were opened as he moved from spiritual blindness to salvation. "Lord, I believe," he said, and bowing before Jesus, he worshiped.

Jesus rarely came right out and said, "I am the Messiah." But the time was at hand for his crucifixion. There was no need to keep the secret any longer.

John Newton caught the pathos of this moment when he wrote:

Amazing Grace, how sweet the sound,
That saved a wretch like me.
I once was lost, but now am found,
Was blind, but now I see.

30

Community

... They broke bread in their homes and ate together with glad and sincere hearts, praising God and enjoying the favor of all the people. ... (Acts 2:46–47)

NOTHING SYMBOLIZES THE SPIRIT of modern Israel as much as the kibbutz. The kibbutzim are farming or industrial communities where people live and work. There are more than 300 kibbutzim in Israel, ranging in size from 200 to 1000 in population. They are found all over the nation. The newest ones are right on the borders—in the areas where heavy fighting once took place.

This morning I'm in a children's playground at Kibbutz Dafna, just a mile from the Lebanese border. Here, on this now peaceful playground, PLO rockets fired from just across the border used to explode almost daily.

The kibbutz residents hold all property in common, with no private ownership of houses, furniture, or automobiles. Meals are eaten in a common dining hall where all community members take turns working. All decisions are made by democratic vote. It is pure communal life.

Today's Israeli kibbutz has much of the flavor of the early church. The Greek word in the Bible for Christian community or fellowship is *koinonia*. That's what the early church was—a family of brothers and sisters. That church is described in Acts 2: "All the believers were together and had everything in common. Selling their possessions and goods they gave to anyone as he had need.... They broke bread in their homes and ate together with glad and sincere hearts."

In 1908, twelve young Jews from eastern Europe immigrated to what was then called Palestine. They settled on a barren, treeless hillside in a place called Dgania—where the Jordan River exits the Sea of Galilee. They were determined to prove to themselves—and to the world—that Jews could return to their roots and make a living off the land. They were the first pioneers of the kibbutz movement.

Following the War of Independence in 1948, many new kibbutzim started as thousands of Jews arrived from all over the world. Some, while believing in communal life, wanted to maintain private ownership. They started other communities called moshavs. Last week I visited a moshav in the Negev Desert where the residents are farming and turning the desert green by raising vegetables under plastic in the scorching desert sun.

Turning Israel green began at Kibbutz Dgania. The Galilean hills were without trees at the beginning of this century. Now much of the nation is covered with forests. Each year all Israelis join in the ceremony of planting trees throughout the nation.

There are few sights more inspiring than listening as a hundred children recite the "Prayer of Planting" as they stick their little trees into the earth of Israel.

Thou who buildest Zion and Jerusalem
Take pleasure in Thy land
And bestow upon it Thy goodness
And Thy grace.

Give dew for a blessing
And cause beneficent rains

To fall in their season,
To satiate the mountains of Israel
And her valleys,
And to water thereon
Every plant and tree,
And these saplings
Which we plant before thee this day.

Make deep their roots
And wide their crown,
That they may blossom forth in grace
Amongst all the trees in Israel,
For good and for beauty.

And strengthen the hands
Of all our brethren,
Who toil to revive the sacred soil
And make fruitful its wastes.
Bless, O Lord, their might,
And may the work of their hands
Find favour before Thee.

Look down from Thy holy habitation,
From heaven,
And bless this land
That it may flow again
With milk and honey.

Amen!

Sitting here among these Jerusalem pines in the Holy Land I realize that's the prayer I want God to answer in my life as well: "May the work of my hands find favour before Thee."

31

A Man's Man

The LORD God took the man and put him in the Garden of Eden to work it and take care of it. (Gn 2:15)

GALILEE IS ALSO REFERRED TO IN THE Bible as the Sea of Tiberias, the latter a reference to the city of Tiberias located midway on the western shore.

In Jesus' day Tiberias was a brand new city, built over the ruins of the Old Testament city of Chinnereth. It was constructed by Herod Antipas and named for the Roman emperor at the time. The most popular spot in the city was the thermal bath—hot springs which flowed from ancient volcanic rock. The city was completed in A.D. 25, just five years before Jesus began his public ministry.

Modern Tiberias is one of the most popular tourist spots in Israel. Herod, a renegade Jew who was trying to please the Jews as well as the Roman overlords, constructed a magnificent synagogue in the center of town. However, since he built over an ancient Jewish cemetery, it was considered unclean by the Jews. Under Jewish law no Jew was permitted to enter the city limits. Therefore, in Jesus' day, Tiberias was inhabited totally by gentiles. There is no evidence that Jesus—who obeyed the Jewish law unless it interfered with God's plan for his life—ever entered the city.

When Jesus left Nazareth to begin his public ministry, he moved to Capernaum, a fishing village located on the north edge of the Sea of Galilee ten miles around the lake from Tiberias. A city of almost 10,000 residents, Capernaum was his home during the last three years of his life on earth. He performed more miracles here than in any other place.

The people of Capernaum, however, refused to respond to his ministry. Therefore Jesus cursed the city along with two nearby towns—Chorazin and Bethsaida. Unlike Tiberias which has continued to flourish until this day, all three of these cities were eventually destroyed and no longer exist. Only a few ruins along the shore give any evidence of the grandeur that was once Capernaum.

Most of Jesus' disciples were fishermen from the villages around the shore of the Sea of Galilee. They fished at night, just as the fishermen of today. Sometimes Jesus would go out with them, spending the night in one of their boats, helping them row and pull their nets.

The nets were heavy, bulky, made of hemp rope which rotted when wet. They were quite unlike the lightweight nylon nets used today. Much of the time was spent mending the nets, which often broke when loaded with fish. During the day, while some of the men were hanging out the nets to dry and repair, the other men would unload the fish and take them to the market. Jesus would help his friends pull the nets from the boat, unload the fish, and take them to market.

I grew up with what I now realize was a bad image of Jesus. Everything I knew about him was based on some really poor pictures I had in my Bible, or on some artist's conception of what he looked like in the little papers I was given at Sunday school. Jesus was always depicted as ultra-serious, effeminate, sunken-eyed, and hollow-cheeked. Maybe it's because the artists all looked like that. I don't know.

But after being here in Israel and seeing what it takes just to stay alive—even 20 centuries later—I realize this man was no sissy. He was a tough, weather-beaten, callous-handed laborer—a "blue-collar worker," so to speak—who knew what it was like to put in a hard day's, or hard night's, work.

Jesus did not see work as a curse, something to be avoided. He saw it as a way of life. An opportunity to provide for himself and for others. Hard work to Jesus was honorable. Only the lazy didn't work. He would have approved of what Paul wrote to the Christians in Thessalonica: "If you don't work, you don't eat."

After a night of fishing, these rugged fishermen would pull their heavy boats up on shore. They would unload their fish and then spend much of the day caulking seams and replacing rotted planks. It was a never-ending job.

Several years ago, when the water in the Sea of Galilee was unusually low, archaeologists discovered an ancient fishing boat buried in the mud. Preserved across the years, it is the same kind of boat used by Peter, James, and John when they fished these waters almost 2,000 years ago. The boat—which is officially called The Boat—is located in a museum on the Jewish kibbutz of Nof Ginossar.

You don't take a twenty-foot boat made of heavy timbers which weighs several thousand pounds out on the lake for a pleasure cruise. When the wind was blowing they might hoist a sail. But most of the time they rowed. Can you imagine four men rowing a boat like this across a lake the size of the Sea of Galilee? Yet Jesus and his disciples often did just that. They were strong men. Rugged men. Outdoors men.

Although Jesus was God, he was also man. All man. And when he was crucified, his strong young body nailed to a cross, he died like a man—in horrible pain. Yet Jesus died, as he lived, for all mankind.

Walking across this small land, following the footsteps of Jesus, has made many truths more real to me. For one, Jesus was a Jew. I've come to realize I cannot really appreciate him until I appreciate his Jewishness. For another, Jesus was a man. A man's man. Understanding that has given me a profound appreciation of his Lordship over my life.

Jesus knows what it's like to sweat, to be tired, to work, to be discouraged. He understands our problems. Jesus cares and helps us shoulder the load.

32

Law and Love

"You nullify the word of God by your tradition that you have handed down. . . ." (Mk 7:13)

JESUS SPENT MUCH OF HIS TIME poking holes in religious balloons. Religion is man's way of trying to please God. On the other hand, Christianity—the word we use to describe the faith of those of us who follow Christ—is God's revelation of himself to mankind. God does not love us because of what we do. He loves us in spite of what we do.

This morning I'm back on the Mount of Beatitudes, overlooking the Sea of Galilee. When I get weary of the commercialism in Jerusalem, the infighting between all the Christian groups, or the impossibility of dealing with the Orthodox Jews because of their stubborn and unbending approach to life, I come back to Galilee. Jesus spent a lot of time teaching in this area. Most of his teaching was with stories. Parables.

Once he told the story of a son—we call him the prodigal son—who left home and wasted his inheritance in riotous living. While we see the parable as the story of a repentant son, Jesus told it to emphasize the love of a father who each day would enter his watchtower in his vineyard—much like the one I wrote about earlier. From that vantage point the father stood, watching, longing for his son to come home.

Another time Jesus told the story of a merchant who came along that notorious road between Jerusalem and Jericho. The man was attacked by thieves who robbed him, beat him, and left him for dead. In Jesus' story two religious Jews passed him by. Then a hated Samaritan, whom the Jews considered a heretic, stopped, rendered aid, took him to an inn, and paid the victim's bill. We call that story the Parable of the Good Samaritan.

We forget, however, that these wonderful stories infuriated the religious Jews. From the very beginning of his public ministry, they made plans to kill Jesus. They couldn't afford having someone like him around who kept upsetting their lifestyle and the way they believed.

Then reports came that Jesus was not only telling stories which encouraged religious change, but was deliberately breaking some of the Jewish laws.

Once when Jesus was teaching near here, an entire delegation of Pharisees—fundamentalist religious Jews— came all the way from Jerusalem, about eighty miles away, to accuse him of heresy—breaking religious laws. Mark tells the story in the seventh chapter of his Gospel.

"The Pharisees and some of the teachers of the law who had come from Jerusalem gathered around Jesus and saw some of his disciples eating food with 'unclean'—that is, ceremonially unwashed—hands."

The Pharisees, like the Orthodox Jews in Jerusalem who still wash their hands before they eat in a modern restaurant, believed they were unclean before God unless they went through a ceremonial washing prior to eating. They also washed their hands before the Sabbath dinner in the home and insisted that the cups, kettles, and plates all go through a ceremonial washing.

So when the Pharisees arrived to complain about Jesus' parables, they found something even worse going on. They demanded an explanation.

Jesus ripped back, "Isaiah was right when he prophesied about you hypocrites; as it is written: 'These people honor me with their lips, but their hearts are far from me.' ... You have let go of the commands of God and are holding on to the traditions of men" (Mk 7:6, 8).

That's tough talk.

To illustrate this, Jesus quoted one of the Ten Commandments: "You insist people honor their father and mother. You Pharisees, however, forbid people from helping their parents—no matter how great the need—with money that has been dedicated to God." Jesus said that was what money dedicated to God should go for—not to line the pockets of the religious leaders.

The practice of dedicating money to God was called Corban. The Corban was money or property given to God, but held in trust by the offerer during his lifetime. Thus a person might declare his business Corban, but continue to use the profits for his own benefit until he died.

The Pharisees, however, said that profits from Corban could only go to the temple and could not be used to help aged or needy parents. An even bigger sin would be to sell the property and use the proceeds to help aging parents.

Jesus had no tolerance for this kind of teaching and lashed out at the Pharisees. "You nullify the word of God by your tradition that you have handed down."

God never honors any law or tradition that causes people to be cruel, unkind, or violate his larger purpose of love.

Jesus was revealing the essential flaw in legalistic religion—which demands we serve rules, rather than having rules which serve us. By shifting attention from God's purpose to our own rules, we sooner or later misuse the rules and violate God's intentions. Jesus struck hard at this and said the law is only fulfilled when we love God with all our heart and love our neighbor as much as we love ourselves.

33

Confession

If we confess our sins, he is faithful and just and will forgive us our sins and purify us from all unrighteousness. (1 Jn 1:9)

A WHILE BACK, after a certain Christian leader had been publicly humiliated by the revelation of personal moral problems, I had a chance to talk with him. If I told you his name, you'd instantly recognize him for he's well known. He had been through hell and was terribly discouraged, defeated, hopeless. I spent the afternoon with him.

"You are going to emerge from this situation preaching about a different kind of God than the one you have known," I told him. "The God you knew was a stern God, a harsh God, a God who punished his children when they fell. You are about to meet the real God. The God who loves his children, who helps those who fall. The God who is for us, not against us."

This is the God Jesus came to teach us about. The longer I am over here in Israel, walking the land where he walked, studying these ancient biographies we know as Matthew, Mark, Luke, and John, the more I am convinced he is a God of love and mercy toward those who fall.

The Jews of Jesus' day believed they had to do certain

things to please God. We still have a lot of Christians who believe that.

Last night at the western wall I watched the Orthodox Jews wrapping their arms and heads with the phylacteries—those little boxes containing portions of Scripture. They do it not only because the Bible commands it to be done—"tie them as symbols on your hands and bind them on your foreheads"—but because they believe God will not love them unless they do.

The door of every orthodox home must have a mezuza—a small replica of a Torah box fastened to the doorpost. Not just to obey the Scripture—"write them on the door frames of your houses and on your gates"—but because they believe God will not love them unless they do.

We have a mezuza on the door frame of our house back home. I put it there in obedience to God's word and as a testimony to all who enter our house that ours is a "house of God." But I do not believe God's love is dependent on my obedience. In fact, his love is unconditional. Paul pointed out that "While we were still sinners, Christ died for us" (Rom 5:8).

I love the mezuza. I kiss my fingers and touch it, as the Jews do, every time I enter my house—symbolic of my love for the law. But my love for the author of the law is so much greater.

In Jesus' day (and among many Jews and even Christians today) to disobey God with any of these things was damning sin. The only way that sin could be forgiven was through a blood sacrifice. Thus once a year, on the Day of Atonement, called Yom Kippur, the chief priest would enter the holy of holies in the temple and offer a prayer of atonement, achieving forgiveness for the people who had made the blood sacrifice.

Jesus came as our sacrificial lamb. When he willingly laid down his life and died for us at Calvary, Jesus became our atonement. From that time on there has been no need for animal sacrifices. In the Book of Hebrews, the author says "It is impossible for the blood of bulls and goats to take away sins. . . . Day after day every priest stands and performs his religious duties; again and again he offers the same sacrifices, which can never take away sins. But when this priest—Jesus—had offered for all time one sacrifice for sins, he sat down at the right hand of God. . . . let us draw near to God with a sincere heart in full assurance of faith, having our hearts sprinkled to cleanse us from a guilty conscience . . ." (Heb 10:4, 11-12, 22).

Jesus tells us that God is not an angry God demanding daily sacrifice. All he wants from us is a repentant and contrite spirit. "If we confess our sins," John wrote to the church, "he (God) is faithful and just and will forgive us our sins and purify us from all unrighteousness" (1 Jn 1:9).

All day I've been wandering around the fields north of the Sea of Galilee, talking with the shepherd children and watching the sheep grazing. It was on a similar day that Jesus was out here with his disciples. Pointing to a group of sheep, Jesus told them a wonderful little story about a good shepherd.

"Suppose one of you has a hundred sheep and loses one of them. Does he not leave the ninety-nine in the open country and go after the lost sheep until he finds it? And when he finds it, he joyfully puts it on his shoulders and goes home. Then he calls his friends and neighbors together and says, 'Rejoice with me; I have found my lost sheep.' I tell you that in the same way there is more rejoicing in heaven over one sinner who repents than over ninety-nine righteous persons who do not need to repent" (Lk 15:4-7).

As I think about this parable I realize my own need to repent. That, it seems to me, is what brings a smile to God's face—not my "perfect" life. He knew I couldn't keep the Ten Commandments when he wrote them. In fact, I don't believe he gave them to be kept. God gave them to reveal his nature, for everyone of them is a testimony of his character.

But knowing I was incapable, the Father sent his Son to die for me. Pleasing him, therefore, is not so much in keeping the commandments (which I cannot keep), but in accepting Jesus as my Savior and repenting when I sin.

For centuries confession of sin has played a major role in the Catholic church. The ancient confessional, with the priest on one side listening and the penitent on the other side whispering through a small opening, is part of the heritage of millions. Now, however, many people—including Catholics—are realizing that the sacrament of confession is even more effective when done face to face.

This makes it real, one priest told me. "When a person looks me in the eye and says, 'I have sinned, I want God to forgive me,' I can almost hear the angels rejoicing in heaven."

The Vatican is right in opposing any form of repentance which does not emphasize the necessity of individual confession. Acknowledging guilt for one's sins is never easy, especially in our Western society which considers guilt a disabling emotion. Unlike the Jews who felt there could be no forgiveness of sin without elaborate methods, many Christians consider sin a quaint, antiquated concept.

Jesus said sin needs to be forgiven because it damages the sinner. But God's nature is to forgive—and forget. And when a sinner repents, he becomes like one of these sheep now nuzzling my hand: once lost, now restored.

34

Who Do You Say I Am?

"But what about you?" he asked. *"Who do you say I am?"*

(Mt 16:15)

EVERYTHING JESUS DID HAD PURPOSE, including bringing his disciples to this place Banias. This is the location of the old city of Caesarea Philippi, twenty-five miles north of the Sea of Galilee. It was a strange place for Jesus to bring his disciples—a place Jews seldom visited. It was outside the region of Herod Antipas, under the Syrian rule of Herod's brother, Philip—for which the principle city was named: Caesarea, for Caesar; Philipi, for Philip the Tetrarch.

After a two-hour hike down from an ancient Nimrod Crusader castle, I'm sitting on a rock beside a huge spring which flows from the side of a mountain. This is one of the headwaters of the Jordan River. But it has another significance as well. The Greeks believed their god Pan—the god of nature, half man, half goat—was born in the cave from which the spring flows. In fact, for centuries this place was called Panias. However, the locals could not pronounce Panias so they called it Banias—the name which still appears on the maps of Israel.

Outside of Jewish influence, Banias was a hotbed for false gods, a gentile stronghold for all the ancient gods of Syria,

Greece, and Rome. Scattered around this place are the ruins of fourteen temples to Baal—a fierce god who used temple prostitutes and sometimes allowed child sacrifice.

Not too far from here I discovered the remains of a great temple of white marble built by Herod the Great, Philip's father, to honor Caesar as God. The place reeked of ancient religions. Yet it was here, under the shadows of these false gods that a homeless, penniless carpenter—soon to be executed as a common criminal—brought his disciples to ask them the most significant question of all time.

Once you understand the setting you can see how significant the question really was. Deliberately setting himself against the background of the world's religions—in all their history and splendor—Jesus demanded his disciples to compare him with them. This was Jesus' mid-course exam in comparative religion.

"Who do you say I am?" he asked.

It was Peter, the simple fisherman from Galilee, who answered. "You are the Christ, the Son of the living God."

The Greek word *Christos* is the same as the Hebrew word *Messiah*. Both mean "the Anointed One."

"Blessed are you, Simon son of Jonah," Jesus answered. "This was not revealed to you by man, but by my Father in heaven."

Jesus called Peter's insight "revelation knowledge"—knowledge that came straight from God. He then called Simon by a new name—Petra, which is the Greek word for rock. "You are now a rock, and on this rock will I build my church."

There have been all kinds of interpretations of what Jesus meant when he said that to Peter. Roman Catholics believe one thing. Most Protestants another.

But putting that aside, let's look at what else he said. "On this rock I will build my church and the gates of hell will not overcome it." When Jesus used the term "church," he was not referring to a building or even an ecclesiastical organization. The Greek word for church was *ekklesia*. The *ekklesia* was a group of men who had been called out of a city and given special authority. The word literally means "the called out ones." These "called out ones" were the elders of a city—the city fathers—who had been elected or appointed and given authority to run and defend the city. Their meeting place was in the gates of the city.

Many times I've entered the old city of Jerusalem by walking down a flight of wide stone steps and going through the Damascus Gate. There is a great wall which surrounds the old city—a city within the new city of Jerusalem. The Damascus Gate is one of the original, ancient gates through the 15-foot wall. It is bordered on each side by high parapets, elaborately constructed to defend the city against attackers. As you enter the gate you go through an outer gate into an S-shaped antechamber. This chamber could be closed off by a series of other gates. While the enemy might batter down the outside gate, there was no room inside for a battering ram.

In peacetime the gate area was used for two purposes. It was the center of trade. All legal decisions of banking and commerce were made here. This area was also the meeting place for the *ekklesia*—the city fathers. It was the seat of authority and dominion.

Thus when Jesus told Peter that his church would have authority over the gates of hell, he was not talking about going to hell and kicking the gates in. He was talking about authority and government. He meant that Satan's government, composed of the world systems, could not overcome the authority of his church. God's people have dominion over all the world systems and over all of Satan's legions.

What a powerful promise Jesus gave his church. Is it just for leaders? No, that authority belongs to every believer—from the smallest child to the oldest saint. We are the church, and we have full authority over Satan's government.

35

A Friend in Need

"Go," said Jesus, "your faith has healed you." . . . (Mk 10:52)

FROM THE JORDAN VALLEY, the only way to get to Jerusalem is through this desert city of Jericho. I pulled in here just before lunch, having driven down from Galilee. I stopped for lunch at a curbside stand, enjoying some humus and falafel, that wonderful Jewish staple made of crushed chickpea paste rolled and deep fried, then stuffed into pita with salad.

Now I've climbed up on top of the old tel, just north of the the little town. The tel is a high hill where the archaeologists are still digging down into the ruins of the ancient city. Old Jericho lies just north of the present city. It covers fourteen acres and is still being excavated. Recent discoveries have led archaeologists to believe they've uncovered portions of the old wall—the one that came tumbling down when Joshua and his army marched around it. No one else is here, so I'm sitting on a bench in the desert sun, trying to reconstruct in my mind what happened that spring day before Passover when Jesus came through here on his last trip up to Jerusalem.

This journey really is "up." The Dead Sea, which I can see from where I'm sitting, is just six miles to the south. It's 1300 feet below sea level. Jericho, sweltering in high humidity, is the lowest city in the world. Jerusalem, less than twenty miles away, is 2400 feet above sea level. That's a 3,700 foot climb up one of the most dangerous roads in the world, the notorious Jericho Road.

Jesus had been safely ensconced at Betharba, about ten miles from here on the other side of the Jordan. An all-points bulletin had been issued by the Jewish Sanhedrin for his arrest if Jesus ever returned to Judea—the region around Jerusalem. He had fled to Betharba for safety.

Then, two weeks before he was crucified, Jesus received word that he was needed in Bethany—a tiny village just outside the walls of Jerusalem. His friend Lazarus was dying. Jesus knew that if he returned he would be arrested and surely executed. Yet he also knew this was God's time to redeem the world. Jesus told his disciples it was time to go.

Crossing the Jordan River, five miles to the east, they passed through Jericho. A beautiful oasis here at the edge of the Judean wilderness dating back to 3,000 B.C., Jericho is the oldest city in the world.

It still remains a beautiful little oasis. The markets display, year around, a colorful variety of luscious fruit grown in the area: dates, melons, plums, apricots, grapes, oranges, grape-fruit, lemons, bananas, mangos, papayas, and those strange things called pomegranates.

Jericho would have been something like that when Jesus came through here. He would have done what I did at lunch today, stopped at a curbside restaurant to get a bite to eat. Ahead of him lay the dreaded Jericho Road which would take him through the rugged Judean wilderness—a place which abounded with wild animals and bandits. (You remember that wonderful little story Jesus told about the Good Samaritan? It took place along that road. In fact, the ruins of the inn where the Samaritan took the man who had been beaten and robbed can still be seen beside the modern road which climbs steeply up from Jericho.)

Jesus had gained a great deal of popularity by his

teachings and miracles. When he came through here the word spread quickly.

"Jesus is here!"

A large crowd gathered, walking with him through the streets. But as Jesus came to the edge of the city and the crowd started to fall back, he heard someone call his name.

"Jesus, son of David, have mercy on me." Jesus turned. It was a blind beggar named Bartimaeus. The people standing around the old man rebuked him for bothering Jesus. But the man yelled even louder.

Mark tells the story. Jesus stopped and said, "Call him." So they called to the blind man. "Hey, cheer up. On your feet. He's calling you." Throwing his cloak aside, Bartimaeus jumped to his feet and came to Jesus. "What do you want me to do for you?" Jesus asked. The blind man said, "Rabbi, I want to see." "Go," said Jesus, "your faith has healed you." Immediately the beggar received his sight and followed Jesus along the road.

Jesus had much more on his mind than talking to blind beggars when he came through here that day. He was on his way to his crucifixion. The weight of the sins of the world was about to be placed on his shoulders. He would die, that all mankind might be saved.

Yet, even under that great burden, Jesus never turned away from a call for help. In that poignant moment, helping a blind beggar—giving him sight—was more important than anything else in the world.

That's my prayer today. I am such a goal-oriented person, pushing ahead to achieve. I so often run over, or rush by, those along the road who are calling out for help. I don't want to be like that. I want to be like Jesus. So I'm praying that God will place in me the same Spirit he placed in his Son, so I can tell the difference between that which is urgent—like getting to Jerusalem—and that which is important—like stopping to help someone in need.

36

Courage to Follow Jesus

Then Thomas (called Didymus) said to the rest of the disciples, "Let us also go, that we may die with him." (Jn 11:16)

FROM WHERE I AM STANDING on the Mount of Olives you can see all the way across the rugged Judean wilderness to the Jordan River. On a clear day, you can see the Dead Sea shimmering in the sun.

Down there, just beyond the horizon on the other side of the Jordan River, was the little town of Betharba. It was outside the region of Judea, and therefore not under the jurisdiction of either King Herod or the Jewish Sanhedrin. Jesus had been there for several weeks—teaching a group of eager people about the kingdom of God.

Jesus' disciples had begged him not to leave the safety of Betharba. They had hoped they could stay close by him, learning more and more about this wonderful new kingdom he was telling them about—the kingdom of God. But a messenger had come from Bethany, a tiny village just beyond the crest of the Mount of Olives where I'm now standing. Jesus had some dear friends who lived there—people he usually stayed with when he was in this area. Now word had come that Mary and Martha's brother, Lazarus, was critically sick. "Rabbi," the disciples had pleaded, "a short while ago the Jews tried to stone you, and yet you are going back there?"

"Lazarus is dead," Jesus had replied. "I need to go so I can raise him."

No one was sure what was going to happen if Jesus returned to Jerusalem. Yet his disciples knew something significant was about to take place. They knew, by this time, that any man who had the power to raise the dead was more than mortal man. Just a few months earlier they had all agreed with Simon Peter when he had told Jesus: "You are Christos, the Son of the Living God."

Jesus had not denied it. In fact, he had told Peter only God could have given him that revelation. Jesus was indeed the Messiah. The Son of God.

For almost three years they had suspected it. Now they knew. But what kind of Messiah was he? Most Jews believed the Messiah would come as a thundering prophet like Elijah. Maybe he would be another Moses, or perhaps a military leader like Judas the Macabee, who 200 years before had defeated the mighty Syrian army.

Instead, Jesus had spent three years teaching them about an invisible kingdom. He taught them that it was better to forgive than to seek vengeance, better to be a servant than a master, better to have God's approval than this world's riches. Jesus taught them it was not enough to be religious. The Jews were religious but many of them were cruel, godless, self-centered, proud, and without mercy. No, it was right to keep the laws of God, but the purpose of that law was to protect them from the world—which would destroy them.

To the religious Jew everything was wrapped up in keeping the law—such as putting on the phylactery before worship. To be touched by a gentile, or a sinner, made a religious Jew unclean—so he washed his hands before worship to cleanse himself of all contamination. They pulled their garments around them to protect themselves from corruption from without, not knowing that true corruption comes from within.

Jesus, on the other hand, mingled freely with commoners. He was more at home with them than with royalty. And certainly more comfortable than with stuffy, religious people who did nothing but talk about how pious they were. He enjoyed sitting with friends, laughing, asking about their families, listening to their stories and, when they were ready, teaching them simple lessons about God.

All this irritated the religious Jews, especially the Sanhedrin, the ruling body. They were threatened by Jesus. He healed on the Sabbath—breaking their laws. He touched lepers—making himself ceremonially unclean. Angry, they began making plans to kill him, not knowing they were part of God's great plan for the universe that the Son of God must die to save the world—to save us—from the consequences of sin.

The disciples, therefore, were confused when Jesus said he had no choice but to leave the safety of Betharba and go up to Jerusalem. They knew and loved Lazarus also. They knew Jesus had the power to raise him from the dead. Yet they also knew if Jesus returned to Jerusalem, he would be facing certain death. What should they do?

It was Thomas, one of his disciples—the one we unfortunately remember as doubting Thomas—who convinced the other disciples. In a powerful statement of raw courage and commitment to his Lord he said, "Let us also go, that we may die with him."

That kind of courage still challenges me. And after climbing the Mount of Olives to the little village of Bethany, I'm once again asking myself: Would I have gone with him, or would I have stayed in the safe place? Will I deny Jesus? Or will I follow him, even if it means losing all I have to gain eternity? I can only pray I'll prove courageous when faced with the decision.

37

Is There Life after Death?

..."Our friend Lazarus has fallen asleep; but I am going there to wake him up." (Jn 11:11)

THE OLDER I GROW the more important the question becomes. "If a man dies, will he live again?" It's the question which wrenches at the heart of us all, starting with Job who first asked it. "Is there life after death?"

On a sunny afternoon in April, right here in the little village of Bethany, just outside the walls of Jerusalem, Jesus answered that question with a resounding yes!

Not many people come here. Bethany isn't really a village anymore. It's on the backside of the Mount of Olives, hidden among the groves of olive trees, at the very edge of the desert hills. In fact, the top of the Mount of Olives is the dividing line between the lush, green part of Israel where the rain falls, and the desert which begins and stretches without sign of human habitation all the way to the Dead Sea. But there's only one thing here that interests me: the tomb of Lazarus.

The story began when Martha, and her tenderhearted sister, Mary, realized their brother Lazarus was dying. They sent desperate word to Jesus—who was more than a day's journey away—begging him to come. They knew he had the power to heal. They had seen him perform miracles many times. Now *they* needed one.

To get here from Betharba, on the far side of the Jordan River, Jesus had to walk almost thirty miles through the Judean wilderness, up one of the steepest and most treacherous roads in the Middle East—the notorious Jericho Road. He arrived about noon the week before the Jewish Passover began.

Jesus had deliberately delayed his arrival. He knew, before he left, that Lazarus had already died. But that was not the real reason for waiting. Jesus had something much bigger in mind than healing his old friend. The time for his crucifixion was at hand. Jesus knew that it was time to lay down his life as a ransom for the world. He needed to make a statement, to demonstrate exactly who he was so no one could misunderstand that he was the Son of God. Jesus was going to raise Lazarus from the dead.

At least twice before Jesus had raised people from the dead. Both were children—the daughter of Jairus and the son of a poor widow in Nain. But in both cases the skeptics had said the children were only sleeping, or in a coma. Knowing that within a week he himself was going to die and be raised from the dead, Jesus used this circumstance to convince the people, once and for all. Not only was he the Messiah, but all authority had been given to him—even authority over death. Jesus was going to raise a man from the dead—a man who had been dead four days, a man whose body had been wrapped in grave clothes and sealed in a below-ground tomb.

Martha met Jesus here at the tomb where they had buried her brother. That's where I am today, sitting on a square rock outside the entrance to this cave-like opening in a rock wall. There's a little Arab shop across the narrow street where you can buy soft drinks and trinkets. Just down the pavement a group of Palestinian children are laughing and tossing rocks at an Orange Crush can. Life goes on as if what happened in this hole never happened. But it did. And it changed the course of history.

Burial in Israel has always been difficult because the land is so rocky. Poor people buried their loved ones on top of the ground. The corpse would be wrapped, then covered with stones to keep away the wild animals. Every year, on the fifteenth of February, the Jews would take whitewash and paint the stones which covered the bodies of their loved ones.

It was this custom that caused Jesus to compare the Pharisees with what he called "whited sepulchres." "Woe to you, teachers of the law and Pharisees, you hypocrites! You are like whitewashed tombs, which look beautiful on the outside but on the inside are full of dead men's bones and everything unclean. In the same way, on the outside you appear to people as righteous but on the inside you are full of hypocrisy and wickedness" (Mt 23:27-28).

Pretty harsh language.

Martha was heartbroken. As with many people caught up in grief, she accused her Lord. "If you had been here," she wept, "he would not have died." Such is the nature of grief. It always contains an element of anger and blame.

"If you had . . ." How typical to blame God when things go wrong. But we all do it. Then she added: "But I know that even now God will give you whatever you ask."

Jesus looked at her. "I am the resurrection and the life. He who believes in me will live, even though he dies; and whoever lives and believes in me will never die. Do you believe this?" (Jn 11:25-26).

Martha didn't know what to answer. No one knew anything about life after death. The Romans and Greeks talked about a miserable existence on the other side of the River Styx. The Sadducees, a priestly group of Jews, said there was no resurrection beyond death. The Pharisees believed in it, but called the afterlife Sheol—a shadowy existence of no heaven or hell. When you died you didn't disappear, you went to Sheol.

So Martha answered the only way she knew how: "It's not a matter of what I believe, it's who I believe. I believe you are the Christ—the Son of God."

Jesus, standing there, saw all the people who had come to mourn the death of their friend. He looked at Mary and Martha, Lazarus's sisters. Jesus loved them as his own sisters. They were all weeping. His own eyes filled with tears and suddenly he was weeping with them. His heart was broken—not because Lazarus had died—but because God had so much more for all these people and they could not see it.

"Take away the stone," Jesus ordered.

This tomb is a natural cave in deep rock. A few minutes ago I climbed down several levels to the gravesite which is hewn out of the side of the cave where the body had been placed. It's about thirty feet below the surface. Since then steps have been cut into the floor, a handrail has been added, and a feeble electric light burns in the ceiling. But on that day there were no steps. No rail. No light. Once you were placed here, you never left. This was a place of the dead.

The body of Lazarus had been prepared aboveground. Mary and Martha, pious Jews, had let their friends in the synagogue handle the details. The skin had been washed, then rubbed with spices to keep down the stench of decaying flesh. Then each arm and leg had been wrapped in white gauze—like a mummy. Finally they wrapped the torso, including his neck and head. Then several men, using ropes, had lowered the body to the bottom of this cave. Climbing down, they placed it on this narrow ledge. A thin shroud was placed over the body, a cloth napkin placed over the bound face, and the men climbed back out of the grave. The rock was rolled into place, leaving the body in pitch darkness.

Then, four days later, came a grinding noise far above as the rock was rolled back. And ringing down through this winding passage was the authoritative shout that ever since has echoed into the hearts of all hopeless men and women. It was the shout of Jesus. "Lazarus, come forth."

Someone once remarked there was so much power and authority in that voice that had not Jesus called Lazarus by name, every grave in the universe would have opened.

With a single word, all the processes of death were reversed. Time was turned around. There was a great stirring as life returned to the body—life which was given at the mere word of God.

Lazarus, stumbling in his grave clothes, groped his way toward the voice which had called him. Crawling up these steps he emerged into the warm afternoon sun.

But it was not enough to have life. Lazarus also needed freedom. "Take off his grave clothes and let him go," Jesus laughed. So many of us have experienced life in Christ, but have never tasted the freedom of being filled with the Holy Spirit.

If we can just grasp the fact that God was standing at the entrance to this tomb, then we will be able to understand what Jesus meant when he said, "I am the resurrection and the life." In other words, if I link my life with Jesus, if I allow the Spirit which raised him from the dead to come and live in me, then I, too, will live as Jesus lives.

That's the answer to the question Job asked. To the question I am asking. Because Jesus lives, I shall live also.

38

Jerusalem

Pray for the peace of Jerusalem. . . . (Ps 122:6)

JERUSALEM. THE HOLY CITY. The Eternal City. Despite all the times I've been here, each time I return I feel the same way: awed and filled with reverence. Why? I've been to thousands of cities, some ancient, some modern. But none of them affects me the way this city does. Each time I make the drive from Tel Aviv to Jerusalem, or from Jericho to Jerusalem, I have that same quickening of the pulse, that same shortness of breath.

It's the same feeling I experienced the sunny afternoon I married my wife. Standing in the back room of the little Baptist church in Florida, listening through the door as the organist played "Here Comes the Bride," peeking through the crack and seeing her waiting at the end of the aisle in her flowing white gown. That's the feeling that I have whenever I approach Jerusalem.

Across the centuries it has been destroyed and rebuilt time and time again. Regardless of the destruction, it keeps being resurrected—as God's creations are always resurrected.

The streets of the old city, inside the ancient wall, brim with life. Here, as in the days of Jesus, vendors sell from their tiny curbs. Donkeys, and sometimes a camel, make their way through the narrow, winding passageways. Merchants from all over the Middle East congregate here—haggling, bartering, making deals.

Jerusalem is a marvelous mixture of old and new. Once you step through the Damascus Gate of the city, passing through the city wall, you pass from the first century to the twentieth century. Outside the old city wall are the modern, teeming streets of new Jerusalem. Here today's bankers and politicians meet to decide the economic and military and political fate of the Middle East—decisions which affect the world.

Through the air I can hear the sound of the bells from the Christian shrines which dominate the city—symbols that Messiah has indeed come.

At sundown during Holy Week, the week leading up to Easter, you can hear the bells from the beautiful Garden of Gethsemane—that lovely garden of ancient olive trees just below where I'm standing. Their sound mixes with the sound of the bells from the Dormition Abbey near the flagstone courtyard of the Roman Fortress Antonia where Jesus was tried by the Roman governor, Pontius Pilate.

But the dominant note of the bells is not from the place where he prayed, nor the place where he was tried, but from the black cupola of the Church of the Holy Sepulcher— where many believe Jesus was buried before he rose from the grave.

Early morning of what we now call Palm Sunday, then known simply as the first day of the week—the day following the Sabbath—Jesus left his friends Mary, Martha, and Lazarus in nearby Bethany and climbed to the summit of this mountain, the Mount of Olives, overlooking the city of Jerusalem.

As the sun rose over the Mountains of Moab beyond the Jordan River, Jesus stood where I am now sitting, his eyes taking in the glory of his Father's creation—and the eternal city of Jerusalem which stretched below.

According to Ezekiel it was here, on the Mount of Olives, that the glory of God would be manifest. Zechariah prophesied the second coming of Christ would take place here: "On that day his feet will stand on the Mount of Olives, east of Jerusalem.... Then the LORD my God will come, and all the holy ones with him" (Zec 14:4-5).

The Jews, knowing Jesus had just raised Lazarus from the dead, and now seeing him on the Mount of Olives, believed the long-awaited Messiah had arrived. They crowded around him, shouting "Hosannah"—which means "save now!"

But Jesus, standing here and seeing below him the temple and the towers within the walls of the city, all radiant in the early dawn sunlight, began to weep. The people wanted a political, a military messiah. The kingdom of God is within you, Jesus had told his disciples. So he stood here and wept over the city: "If you, even you, had only known on this day what would bring you peace—but now it is hidden from your eyes" (Lk 19:42).

"Pray for the peace of Jerusalem," David the psalmist wrote. What brings true peace? Not military nor political power. Not money. Not fame. Not hedonistic pleasure. These things bring anxiety—and death. But if you invite Jesus, the living Lord, into your life—he brings peace.

Today, as I sit on the low stone wall on the Mount of Olives, the city is different from the city Jesus saw. But it remains Jerusalem, a city to be revered, a city to be wept over. And I am forced to ask myself: What does he think as he looks at our beautiful churches back in the States, our solemn feasts, our religious assemblies where we, even yet, misunderstand his mission and purpose?

Jesus came to bring us peace, yet we continue to war with each other over various points of doctrine, just as the Jews warred over the interpretation of the law. Have we progressed? We need to weep over the churches, just as Jesus wept over the city of Jerusalem.

39

Riding on a Donkey

They took palm branches and went out to meet him, shouting, "Hosanna!" ... (Jn 12:13)

TODAY IS SUNDAY. The Sabbath ended at sundown last night. The city of Jerusalem, which I can see from my vantage point here on the Mount of Olives, is bustling. It was probably like this that Sunday morning Jesus stood here—the Sunday we now call Palm Sunday.

He had spent the night at the home of Mary, Martha, and Lazarus. There had been something of a banquet in his honor after the Sabbath had ended. Mary had brought out an expensive jar of perfume she had been saving, poured it on his feet, then wiped them with her long hair. Judas, the treasurer of Jesus' little group, objected. He complained it would have been better had she sold the perfume and given the money to the poor. Jesus gently rebuked him, saying the poor would always be around, but she had anointed him for his burial.

It's one of the most poignant and beautiful stories in the Bible, one which I cannot read without having tears come to my eyes.

The next morning Jesus rose at dawn and came out here where I am today, overlooking the city of Jerusalem from the crest of the Mount of Olives. Stretched before him was his destiny—the Holy City, Jerusalem.

As the little town of Bethany was the watershed in the nation of Israel, so the raising of Lazarus from the dead was the watershed in the life of Jesus. From that point on there was no turning back. The Jewish rabbis believed the raising of the dead involved the practice of magic or conjuring. Hearing what had happened, the Jewish high council—the Sanhedrin—issued a proclamation: Jesus was a dangerous man and was to be arrested.

Jesus ignored it. He rose early that Sunday morning and came here to get quiet before God. What mixed emotions he must have had as he stood here, remembering the night before in little Bethany. His closest friends had been there—men with whom he had walked for three years. Some of the women were there also—women who loved him dearly, but were confused and frustrated in expressing their love. For Jesus never responded romantically, only with ultimate kindness.

His disciples finally joined him, wondering what Jesus had planned for the day. He was evasive to their questions. Leaving the summit, he asked them to follow him as he made his way down the narrow Roman road to the city.

Word that Jesus was coming spread quickly. Expecting he was about to announce his messiahship, the people swarmed out from Jerusalem to meet him. Many stood along the street waving palm branches. They shouted, "Hosannah!" They were excited almost to the point of hysteria. The Messiah had arrived—the one who was going to save them from the hated Romans.

Then something changed. Jesus sent his disciples ahead of him, telling them to find a particular donkey he was to ride into the city. Part way down the ancient Roman road which entered the temple courtyard through the Golden Gate, Jesus saw his disciples waiting with the donkey. He stopped and mounted. It was a symbolic move.

Hundreds of years before, the prophet Zechariah had prophesied: "Rejoice greatly, O Daughter of Zion! Shout, Daughter of Jerusalem! See, your king comes to you, righteous and having salvation, gentle and riding on a donkey, on a colt, the foal of a donkey" (Zec 9:9).

The donkey Jesus chose to ride was not the beast of burden now seen in the old city of Jerusalem. The donkey Jesus rode came from a breed now extinct—a tiny wild ass, its back no more than three feet from the ground. The colt had never been saddled before, much less borne a rider.

Jesus must have looked ridiculous sitting on this tiny animal, not much bigger than a large dog, his feet dragging the ground. Yet he straddled it and rode into the city—in meekness and humility. Royalty and military leaders rode on horses. The wealthy merchants rode camels. Only the poor rode donkeys—and no one rode a wild ass. Yet Jesus mounted the colt and continued his slow descent toward Jerusalem.

Some of the people must have wondered, even as they continued to wave their palm branches and shout "Hosannah!" Perhaps they had made a mistake. Most believed the messiah would overthrow the Romans and reestablish Israel as a theocracy like David's. But what kind of messiah would come riding a lowly donkey?

Such an action was typical of Jesus. Some grew disillusioned. Angry. Some who turned out on Sunday to wave branches quickly turned away when they realized Jesus was calling for a different kind of commitment. He was not building an earthly kingdom—but a heavenly one. He challenged them to be kind, forgiving . . . to serve one another. They couldn't handle it. Sadly, many who stood along the road on Palm Sunday shouting "Hosannah" also stood in the courtyard of Pontius Pilate—less than a week later—shouting, "Crucify him!"

Yet the king, riding the donkey, did not turn back. His heart was set. Jesus would obey God whether any stood with him or not. He was ushering in an entirely different kind of kingdom—a kingdom of servants. And Jesus was the one to lead the way.

Am I one of those who stands and waves palm leaves but will not stand with Jesus in the end? Or am I willing to give my life to him as Lord and Savior?

40

When God Makes a Promise

> *"So is my word that goes out from my mouth:*
> *it will not return to me empty,*
> *but will accomplish what I desire*
> *and achieve the purpose for which I sent it."* (Is 55:11)

AFTER LEAVING THE MOUNT OF OLIVES on Palm Sunday, Jesus made his way down the old Roman Road to the wall surrounding the city of Jerusalem. His destination: the temple.

The first temple had been built by King Solomon. It was a magnificent structure dedicated in 950 B.C. and stood for almost 400 years before it was destroyed by the Babylonians. It was rebuilt seventy-two years later when the Jews returned from Babylon. For the next 500 years the city of Jerusalem was under constant siege. The temple was desecrated time and time again until rebuilt by Herod the Great on thirty-five acres inside the eastern wall of Jerusalem.

Jesus entered the city through the Golden Gate which opened through Solomon's Porch into the temple grounds.

The people, who had lined the streets on Palm Sunday shouting "Hosannah," flocked through the gate with him—pouring into the temple grounds. It was an ideal time for Jesus to announce his messiahship. Instead, however, he moved slowly through the temple area, his piercing eyes taking in everything.

No doubt his heart was filled with sadness. When God instituted temple worship during the time of Solomon, he intended for the people to bring their offerings—the first fruits of their crops and herds—to be sacrificed by the priests to atone for their sins. It was a beautiful, simple act.

But temple worship became corrupt. Instead of allowing the people to bring their own lambs, calves, and pigeons to be sacrificed, the religious leaders saw this as a way to make money. They required the people to purchase their animals in the temple. The high priest appointed "temple merchants" —usually family members and friends—to sell the animals at huge profits. It was ultimate corruption.

Jesus saw all this and slowly a great rage built inside him. Picking up a rope used to tether one of the animals, he began flailing the merchants, overturning their tables, and in an explosion of anger shouted that they had turned God's house of prayer into a den of thieves. The merchants fled before him, their pigeons fluttering skyward, their animals fleeing in all directions.

This outburst took everyone by surprise. The people, believing Jesus was the kind of messiah who would over-throw the Romans, were shocked when instead he ripped into the religious leaders and their corrupt ways. The crowd, embarrassed and confused, dissipated. Those who had hoped to use Jesus for their own political gain quickly turned against him. They would need to find another messiah. This one was unmanageable.

I've been sitting here on a rock beside a busy street just outside the Golden Gate. It was through this gate Jesus entered the city. There was deep significance in Jesus' choice to use this entrance. The Golden Gate was reserved for priests to use. Jesus was, and is, our high priest—the one who atoned for our sin.

The Golden Gate is also the gate many believe Christ will use to enter Jerusalem when he comes again—descending from the Mount of Olives. It's not in use any more. It fact, it has not been used since the early middle ages. In the sixteenth century the Turkish sultan, Suleiman, upon learning that Jesus might use this gate to enter the city of Jerusalem when he returns, had it bricked up. A Moslem's way of stopping God.

Other Moslems, and some Jews, knowing the law forbade a Jewish rabbi from walking on a grave, felt they could prevent Christ from entering the city when he returns by burying their dead on the slopes of the Mount of Olives in front of the Golden Gate. Their graves still crowd the area in front of me.

Sultans, kings, dictators—even religious leaders—all have attempted to stop God's plan. No man, however, can brick up the gate through which Jesus wants to enter your life. In that same passage where Isaiah said God's ways are not our ways, nor his thoughts our thoughts, he concluded:

"As the rain and the snow
    come down from heaven,
and do not return to it
    without watering the earth
and making it bud and flourish,
    so that it yields seed for the sower
        and bread for the eater,
so is my word that goes out from my mouth:
    It will not return to me empty,
but will accomplish what I desire
    and achieve the purpose for which I sent it." Is 55:10-11

There's a lot of activity in front of the Golden Gate today. I've been sitting here on this stone beside the road for more than an hour since the sun came up. It's a busy place. Trucks filled with produce, cars taking people to and from work, huge busses filled with gawking tourists—all roar past here on their way to other areas of business and interest. The Golden Gate stands as a silent witness to all this activity.

One day, however, the activity will intensify even more. I don't know whether Jesus is actually going to descend up there on the Mount of Olives when he returns. The angels said he would, but I'm not sure what that actually means. Nor do I know whether he's going to literally enter Jerusalem through this gate. But I do know this: no man will ever stop that wonderful event. And when it comes, I want to be eager and ready.

41

Spiritual Reserves

". . . The kingdom of heaven will be like ten virgins who took their lamps and went out to meet the bridegroom. Five of them were foolish and five were wise." (Mt 25:1–2)

IT WAS THE LAST WEEK OF JESUS' LIFE on earth. By noon Friday he would be dying on a cross outside the city. He was running against a deadline and knew he had only a few hours to finish sharing the principles of the kingdom with his disciples.

Earlier in the day Jesus and his disciples had been up on the Mount of Olives overlooking Jerusalem. Jesus had told them that certain signs would accompany the end of time. He said there would be wars and rumors of wars, that people would grow more wicked, that many of those in the church would become humanistic and fall away. But, Jesus told them, no one knew when the "end of time" would take place—not even the angels.

Coming down they made their way to the house of a wealthy friend in the city and entered the courtyard. That's where I am today. It's not the same courtyard. No one knows where that place was. So many of the places and events in Jesus' life are left to our imagination. Maybe God wants it that way so we can more easily picture him in our town, in our kitchen, rather than in a 2000-year-old house in Jerusalem.

Yet even though we don't know exactly where Jesus was, we know the story he told as vividly recorded in the Bible. It was a simple parable about a wedding feast.

Yesterday noon as I was walking through the crowded streets of the old city—which is like going back 2000 years to the narrow, cobblestone streets with small shops and booths lining the crowded avenues—I spotted a Jewish wedding celebration. A group of about thirty men and women were pushing their way through the crowd, singing and laughing. They were holding aloft a large blue and white striped tent, or pavilion covering. Under it were the bride and groom dressed in their wedding clothes. The wedding party were dancing and singing as they made their way down the street and disappeared around a corner.

The Jews then, like the Jews of today, loved to celebrate weddings. The celebration would begin with a great reception, usually in the home of the bride's father. That was followed by a feast, which was followed by the actual ceremony. Then the couple, just as the couple I saw yesterday, were escorted through the city with singing.

The highlight of these festivities was the coming of the bridegroom, who could show up at any time just before the wedding. In Jesus' story it was after dark when word came that the bridegroom was on his way. Ten of the bridesmaids rushed out of the house to meet him, carrying their little lamps with them to light his way down the road and into the courtyard. These little lamps, with a tiny burning wick, were filled with olive oil.

The groom, however, was delayed for some reason. The young women sat on the side of the road, waiting, and finally fell asleep. At midnight they heard him coming. They picked up their lamps only to discover the oil had burned out.

Five of the bridesmaids had brought extra oil for their

lamps. They quickly trimmed their wicks, then refilled their lamps from the jar of reserve oil they had brought. The other five had no reserve oil. They begged the others to share, but the girls said, "There is not enough. You should have brought your own reserves. You'll have to go out and buy some."

But it was too late. While the foolish bridesmaids were out searching for oil, the bridegroom showed up. He took the five wise bridesmaids, entered the house, and locked the gate behind him.

Finishing his story, Jesus looked at his disciples. "Therefore, keep watch, for you do not know the day or the hour."

For years, when I read this story, I thought Jesus used the five wise bridesmaids to represent Christians. The five foolish ones—those who didn't have oil for their lamps, I thought represented those who didn't believe in Jesus. But now I understand that was not the case. It's not that the five foolish girls had no oil. Rather, they had oil only in their lamps. They had no reserves.

All the girls had oil to start with. The lamps were all lit in the early part of the evening. But Jesus was saying, "It's not enough to be a Christian—to be a member of the wedding party, a member of my church. You need reserve oil. You need to be filled with the Holy Spirit as well."

It was a theme, an overpowering emphasis that Jesus hammered on constantly during that last week of his life—the week we call the "passion week." It was as if he had saved the most important things until the last. There had been little need to emphasize the importance of receiving the Holy Spirit up until now. But now, with his departure so close, almost everything Jesus said emphasized the necessity of being filled with the Holy Spirit.

This means I have to ask myself the question Jesus asked his disciples "Do I have spiritual reserves? What will happen to me when the crisis comes? Will I stand or will I fall?"

When the crunch came for the disciples, none of them

stood with Jesus—even though all had sworn they would never desert him. One of them, Judas, actually betrayed him. But fifty days after the crucifixion—on the Day of Pentecost—those same fearful disciples had their lamps filled. They were filled with the Holy Spirit and became bold, daring, fearless witnesses for Jesus Christ.

Jesus told this little parable the week before he was crucified to teach his followers that it's not enough to belong to his church. It's not enough to praise him. A lot of people did that on Palm Sunday, lining the streets shouting "Hosannah." But when the crisis came, they were nowhere to be found. Their lamps had run out of oil.

An old Pentecostal friend of mine used to say, "What we Christians need to do is stay under the spout where the glory runs out." He's right. That's what Paul meant when in the Book of Ephesians he said, "Be ye filled, and filled, and filled, and filled with the Holy Spirit."

42

Bread and Wine, Towel and Basin

"Now that I, your Lord and Teacher, have washed your feet, you also should wash one another's feet." (Jn 13:14)

S O MUCH WAS CROWDED INTO those last few days of Jesus' life before his crucifixion. More than half of the Gospel of John is spent detailing the events of the last week of his life on earth. John describes what happened in a place called the Upper Room, on the Thursday night before Jesus was crucified.

Jesus had sent Peter and John into the city saying, "Go and make preparations for us to eat the Passover" (Lk 22:8).

"Where do you want us to prepare for it?" they asked.

"As you enter the city, a man carrying a jar of water will meet you. Follow him to the house that he enters, and say to the owner of the house, 'The Teacher asks: Where is the guest room, where I may eat the Passover with my disciples?' He will show you a large upper room, all furnished. Make preparations there."

Sitting here on a window ledge in the traditional Upper Room just outside the wall of the old city of Jerusalem, I'm aware this is not the same room where Jesus brought his disciples to eat the Passover meal. I'm no student of architecture, but I recognize these columns and arches as Byzantine, from the period of the Crusaders. However, it was a room similar to this where Jesus took the Passover elements and consecrated them with a new meaning. The actual place is unimportant. All that counts is that Jesus took bread and said, "My body, broken for you"; then took the cup and said, "My blood, shed for you."

As I sit here the room has now filled with pilgrims. Many of them come daily—from all over the world—to take holy communion in remembrance of him—a sacrament which Jesus himself instituted, perhaps in this very place. Sitting here I've watched half a dozen small groups come and go. They've stood silently, heads bowed, praying. Each group has taken communion—all in different languages.

Their love for Jesus has touched me deeply.

The first group was Norwegian, the women's heads wrapped in scarves, the men tall and blond. A rugged young pastor was in their midst, his blue eyes dancing as he read the familiar words of the Eucharist in his language.

Next came the Germans who stood in one corner—stiff and straight—while a group of Dutch Christians knelt in the center of the room. Their languages were a beautiful blend. I thought of my last visit to Holland. I had stood in the square in Putten where the Dutch had placed a statue in memory of the heartbroken "widows of Putten." It was here, in the early years of World War II during the Nazi occupation of the Netherlands, that the Germans had executed all the men in the village in retaliation against the Dutch underground. Now I'm watching Dutch and Germans meeting peacefully together in the Upper Room in Israel. I am reminded that true peace is found only in Jesus.

A large band of Pentecostals from South Africa mixed with a group of Roman Catholics from Mexico. They joined hands around the room, forming a large circle. They sang a charismatic chorus—the Africans singing in Afrikans and the Mexicans in Spanish. I sang quietly along with them—in English.

Sitting here I've heard Tagalog from the Philippines, Swahili from Kenya, and Portuguese from Brazil. I was here one day when a group of aborigines from New Guinea stood in the corner, weeping with joy, as their tribal leader read the communion service from the Book of Common Prayer in Pidgin English.

How ironic that the most meaningful sacrament of the church is the one area which separates Christians from one another. Yet one truth is shared by all. What Jesus did in this room the night before he was crucified had eternal significance. For it was on that night, in this place, that the old covenant was fulfilled, and a new promise was made to the church. "This is my body, given for you; do this in remembrance of me. . . . This cup is the new covenant in my blood, which is poured out for you."

At the close of the meal Jesus took the leftover bread and served it to his followers. "This is my body," he said, "broken for you."

Then Jesus took the Passover cup with the remainder of the wine and passed it among them. "This is my blood shed for you," he said openly, "as often as you drink it, do it in remembrance of me."

They had no idea what he was talking about. But they would remember—and in the days ahead it would all make sense.

Then picking up the basin and towel left by the servant who had washed their feet when they came in, Jesus started around the room—washing the feet of each disciple. When he finished he said, "Now that I, your Lord and Teacher have washed your feet, so you should wash one another's feet."

I've watched Christians for a long time. I've concluded some of them serve because they have to. Jesus, on the other hand, served because he wanted to.

John is specific with the record: "Jesus knew that the

Father had put all things under his power . . . so he got up
from the meal, . . . wrapped a towel around his waist, . . . and
began to wash his disciples' feet.''

Aside from his willingness to go to the cross, nothing gives
us any more dramatic picture of the kind of people God
wants us to be—a people who serve one another.

What does that night say to us? Taking his body and
blood, broken and shed for us, we remember. Picking up the
towel and basin, we wash one another's feet and indicate
our role in life—servanthood.

43

The Last Supper

"All this I have told you so that you will not go astray." (Jn 16:1)

THE LAST WEEK OF JESUS' life was filled with drama. No wonder church historians refer to it as the passion week. All the events of time were rushing toward one mighty climax.

Jesus had been safe as long as he remained in the northern region of Galilee. Even though he had met opposition, he knew that the sinister forces in the southern region of Israel would not come north to harm him. Yet as the time for the Passover approached, Jesus knew his time was at hand. The Bible says that against the advice of his disciples, Jesus "resolutely set his face toward Jerusalem."

The night of the Passover meal, Jesus and his disciples met in an upper room in the city of Jerusalem to eat the ritual dinner. Jesus knew it was the last night of his life. He wanted to spend it with his friends—those to whom he was committing the entire ministry of the kingdom of God. That room, later called the *Cenacle*, taken from the Latin word for dining room, was a place where friends could dine in private. Jesus had arranged it so he could be alone with his twelve disciples—men into whom he had poured his life for the last three years.

Jesus had arrived in Jerusalem on Sunday, but each evening had returned to the little village of Bethany, just outside the city walls. There he spent the nights with his friends, Lazarus, Mary, and Martha who provided a pallet for him on the floor of their humble house. On Tuesday night Jesus had quietly slipped out of the house and gone, alone, to a spot on the nearby Mount of Olives. When his disciples saw that he was gone, they went looking for him. In the shadows of an olive grove, they saw their teacher sitting alone, deep in thought.

As they had done so often in the past, they gathered at his feet and spoke of things that were troubling them. One of them was curious about the rumor that had circulated all afternoon that the temple would be destroyed. "Tell us," he asked, "when will this be, and what will be the sign of your coming and of the close of the age?"

They knew Jesus was the Messiah. But they were confused as to what kind of Messiah he was. "Messiah" to them meant something much different than it means to us. They, too, had gotten caught up in the militant Palm Sunday excitement, shouting "Hosannah!"—"Save Now!"—as Jesus entered the city. Now, even though they loved him, they were confused.

Looking around at their attentive faces, Jesus must have felt a twinge of sadness at the thought that he would soon leave them. Would these men, with whom he had shared the secrets of the kingdom of God, be able to carry on his mission without him? Yet there was a quiet confidence—for Jesus knew that even though he was leaving, they would not be alone. That mysterious, but very real, third person of the Trinity—the Holy Spirit—would come and fill them. Jesus knew, but they didn't.

"You know that after two days the Passover is coming, and the Son of Man will be delivered up to be crucified," he said tenderly.

There. He had said it. Yet somehow it didn't register.

Neither would they comprehend what Jesus meant when he said to them two nights later in the upper room, "But after I have risen, I will go ahead of you into Galilee."

"Risen?" You see, they had no frame of reference. Resurrection from the dead was as foreign, as ridiculous, as if he had said, "After I've become a butterfly I'll light on your head." They thought Jesus was talking in riddles, in parables.

The mood was solemn that Thursday night as they took the Passover together. Old friends, yet not so old. Jesus was only thirty-three. The other men were mostly in their late twenties or early thirties. How could they comprehend? Only Jesus was aware of the great drama which was being played out in the heavenlies—and on earth.

Even as they met to take the Passover meal, the chief priest and elders of the Sanhedrin were gathering at the palace of Caiaphas, the high priest, to discuss Jesus' fate. Ironically, that house stood just a block or so from the house where Jesus and the disciples were meeting in the upper room.

Those religious leaders knew there were no legitimate grounds to arrest Jesus. They had tried in every way to get him to blaspheme God, to break the law of Moses. But Jesus knew the law far better than they—after all, he had dictated it to Moses. He knew more than the law: Jesus knew the reason behind it. It was impossible to trap him. The only way to get rid of him was on a fraudulent charge. All they needed was a traitor from his camp who would tell them where Jesus could be found. They found one in Judas.

That night every Jew in the city was eating the same meal—the meal commemorating the exodus of the Jews from Egypt when the death angel passed over the houses that had been marked with the blood of a lamb.

However, unknown to everyone but Jesus himself, a new Passover was taking place. The next day the Lamb of God would be slain on a cross outside the city wall, fulfilling the prophecy spoken by John the Baptist three years before: "Behold, the Lamb of God who takes away the sin of the world."

The last of his biographers, the apostle John, writing from the Isle of Patmos almost sixty years later, summarized it for us: "He was in the world, and though the world was made through him, the world did not recognize him. He came to that which was his own, but his own did not receive him. Yet to all who received him, to those who believed in his name, he gave the right to become children of God."

44

Gethsemane

*Then Jesus went with his disciples to a place called Geth-
semane. . . .* (Mt 26:36)

GETHSEMANE. What thoughts the word brings to mind.
Olive trees. Jesus kneeling beside a great rock—
praying. Sweat mixed with blood falling to the ground.
"Lord, if it be thy will let this cup pass from me; nevertheless,
not my will but thine be done." For the millions of
Christians around the world who worship our Lord, this is
one of the most important sites in biblical history.

It's quiet up here tonight. There's a half moon hanging in
the sky above the old city, whose walls are bathed in soft
floodlights. It's Shabbot, Friday evening, so the traffic has
virtually stopped. There's an ancient church built on the
traditional site of Gethsemane and thousands of visitors
walk quietly through the gardens each day, but the olive
trees remain—possibly the same ones that were here when
Jesus came that fateful night and cried out to his Father.

I wanted to wait until the crowds were gone. I'm
uncomfortable trying to hear God, even worship him, in the
middle of a mob of milling, unruly people. So I waited until
after sundown to arrive. I needed these few moments of

solitude. The Garden was locked so I walked on up the steep hill through an old olive grove. I found this old stone wall and have been sitting here next to the gnarled trunk of a huge, old olive tree, trying to figure out what Gethsemane should mean to me in my own spiritual pilgrimage.

Gethsemane, however, was only one step along the path for Jesus—a path which led to Calvary. His final trip began Thursday night at sundown when Jesus and his friends met in the upper room in Jerusalem to celebrate the Passover meal.

From there they made their way through the darkened city streets of Jerusalem to the gate in the wall. Some place along the way they probably split up, to keep from drawing attention to themselves. They agreed to meet at their accustomed place on the Mount of Olives.

As they were walking, Jesus talked to his disciples—using every valuable minute to teach them about the kingdom of God. Passing a small vineyard on the side of the hill, he said, "I am the vine; you are the branches. If a man remains in me and I in him, he will bear much fruit" (Jn 15:5).

As they walked through the darkness they passed the high wall surrounding the temple—called "the pinnacle of the temple." Three years before Satan had tempted Jesus to throw himself off the pinnacle. "God has promised to send his angels to keep you from harm and death," Satan had taunted.

Now Jesus was faced with an even greater decision. Would God protect him from an agonizing death on the cross? Jesus knew the answer. Turning to his disciples, Jesus said, "It is for your good I am going away. Unless I go away the Counselor will not come to you, but if I go I will send him to you."

Jesus knew. He knew he was going to be crucified. But if Jesus died, then the Holy Spirit would be set free in the world. "I have much more to say to you, more than you can now bear. But when he, the Spirit of truth, comes, he will guide you into all truth ... Greater things than I have done will you do, because I go to my Father."

Turning to his right, Jesus descended into the Kidron Valley, then climbed the hill on the other side to an olive grove where I am tonight. There was a full moon, and the grove was bathed in soft light. A gentle breeze stirred the gray green leaves on the ancient trees.

Jesus looked sadly at his twelve followers seated around him. "You will all fall away because of me this night . . ." Peter stood to his feet, shaking his rugged head. They were about the same age—early thirties. What kind of talk was this? They had been through too much together for Peter to desert his friend.

"Even if all fall away on account of you, I never will," Peter growled.

Jesus just looked at him. "I tell you the truth, this very night, before the rooster crows, you will disown me three times."

Peter replied: "Even if I have to die with you, I will not disown you." Taking Peter, James, and John with him, Jesus pulled aside.

Sitting on an old stump, he opened himself to them in a way he never had before. Always, in every situation, the disciples had found him fearless. But tonight things were different. The disciples could sense it.

"My soul is overwhelmed with sorrow to the point of death," Jesus said. He was not afraid—just terribly burdened.

Pleading, he asked, "Stay here and keep watch with me."

But they quickly dropped off to sleep. Going on alone, Jesus fell to his knees and prayed that prayer which shook the world: "Father, if you are willing, take this cup from me; yet not my will, but yours be done" (Lk 22:42).

It was over the moment Jesus prayed. Other events

followed in quick order. His betrayal by Judas. His arrest, trial, and crucifixion. But it all hinged on that powerful prayer of relinquishment. God's will, not mine.

That's the answer to my question—to all my questions. Relinquishment to his will.

45

The Via Dolorosa

. . . Then they led him away to crucify him. (Mt 27:31)

TODAY IS GOOD FRIDAY. I'm standing in the old city of Jerusalem. Above me is a small street sign which tells it all. *Via Dolorosa.* It means: "The Way of Sorrows."

This is the traditional path Jesus followed as he carried his cross from Pilate's judgment hall to Calvary. Since then this street has been walked by millions of pilgrims.

The night Jesus was arrested in the Garden of Gethsemane, he was brought into the old city to be tried. It was quick. Too quick. His arrest took place after midnight and by dawn the officials had met, tried, and sentenced him to death. Jesus was shuffled back and forth between the Jewish high priest, King Herod, and finally the Roman governor, Pontius Pilate, who pronounced the death sentence.

No one is really sure where it all took place, for most of the buildings were knocked down when the city was destroyed by Rome in A.D. 70. However, somewhere under the pavement of these streets lies the original Way of the Cross.

Each Friday at 3 P.M., Franciscan priests lead pilgrims along the Via Dolorosa. Today, in several hours, this place will be teeming with more than 100,000 pilgrims who will follow a huge cross being carried by many people as they retrace

Jesus' footsteps. I'm not interested in being part of that massive procession, so I've come here at dawn to make my own pilgrimage on this, the traditional day my Lord was crucified.

A Moslem school has replaced the praetorium or Pilate's judgment hall. The place is marked in this narrow street by this arch. Here Pontius Pilate turned to the crowd waiting in the courtyard and said in Latin, "Ecce homo"—"Behold the man." The chief priests then led the mob in shouting, "Crucify! Crucify!" God, let me be one who stands with Jesus—not against him.

Opposite the praetorium is the place where Jesus was flogged and a crown of thorns was placed on his head. This pavement is the actual courtyard of Herod's fortress called the Antonia. "They clothed him in a purple robe and went up to him again and again, saying, 'Hail, King of the Jews!' They spit on him and took a staff and struck him on the head again and again." Lord, forgive me for my own blasphemy.

Jesus, forced to carry his own cross through the city streets, even though weakened by the horrible beatings, stumbled and fell along the way. There's an indentation in the stone wall where people believe he placed his hand. Many who pass here reach out and place their hand in that same print. It's happened so many times across the years the indentation is now deep in the stone. God, I thank you that by the stripes of Jesus I am healed.

Some place as he struggled up these stone steps, Jesus spied his mother, roughly restrained by the Roman soldiers, her anguished face peering from the crowd. God, thank you for the virgin Mary who remains blessed above all women for giving us your son, Jesus, who died for our sins.

The procession turns right into this arched alley. Here Jesus stumbled, bracing himself against the wall. The Roman soldiers spied a black man from Africa in the crowd of onlookers—Simon from Cyrene. They pulled him from the crowd and made him carry the cross for Jesus. Lord, I ask you to give me strength to bear the cross of Jesus.

Legend says that a young woman named Veronica broke from the crowd and ran forward with a cloth, wiping the sweat and blood from Jesus' brow as she wept. Many believe this was the same woman who had been healed by touching the hem of his garment. Today, God, may I help someone in the name of Jesus—and so do it unto him.

I've climbed up a number of large steps through a vaulted alley and have come out into the main market of the old city. Opposite is the gate of judgment—through which Jesus was led out of the city. Just beyond the gate was a skull-shaped hill called Calvary. Lord, may I not pass judgment on anyone—even my enemies. May I forgive and help instead of judging.

If I continued straight up those steps I would reach the place where Jesus turned and spoke to the women who had followed him through the streets, mourning and wailing. "Daughters of Jerusalem," Jesus said, "do not weep for me; weep for yourselves and for your children . . . For if men do these things when the tree is green, what will happen when it is dry." His reference to himself as the "green tree" comes from the prophet Ezekiel and is a bold messianic claim.

On this Good Friday, I commit myself to be a follower of Jesus carrying my own cross along my own Via Dolorosa.

46

Who Killed Jesus?

". . . I lay down my life for the sheep." (Jn 10:15)

WHO KILLED JESUS?
That question has bothered men ever since the time of Calvary. Wars have been fought over it. Crusades have happened because of it. Millions of people have been slaughtered, and millions of others have been treated like outcasts—all because we've failed to understand what really happened that day when Jesus was crucified.

Roman soldiers drove the nails into his hands and feet, raised the cross where Jesus hung until he died, and drove the spear into his side. Yet the soldiers were merely executioners—men following orders to kill a Jewish trouble-maker. In first century Israel it happened frequently. Human life was cheap; the execution of Jesus by the Roman soldiers was just another crucifixion assignment.

But were the Romans the ones who killed Jesus?

Others blamed the Jews. The Jewish leaders conspired to have him arrested and killed. A mob of Jewish people stood in Pilate's courtyard before dawn on that Friday morning and shouted, "Crucify him!"

"Ecce homo," Pilate said, which is Latin for "Behold the man."

Jesus stood before the mob, his hands chained. His back bleeding. A crown of thorns shoved cruelly down over his forehead. It must have been an eerie scene.

This morning, I'm sitting here on the bottom step of a stone stairway inside the wall of the old city of Jerusalem. This street has a little sign on it: Via Dolorosa, the way of sorrows. Just a few feet in front of me are the original flagstones of Pilate's courtyard. It was here, on these stones, the people stood on that early morning just as the sun was coming up over the Judean hills. "Let his blood be on us and on our children," the Jewish leaders cried.

Were they the ones who killed Jesus?

Do they deserve the term that Christians have hung on them across the years: Christ-killers?

But can we really blame the Jews? After all, it was the Roman governor, Pontius Pilate, who actually condemned him to death. Yet Pilate was a weak man. His primary task was to keep peace—to keep the Jews from breaking out in rebellion. No doubt he originally thought of Jesus as a troublemaker, an insurrectionist like that other man condemned to die, Barabbas. Then he met him face to face and realized this man was indeed a prince—a prince of peace.

Pilate tried to absolve himself from guilt by saying, "The man has committed no crime."

"Crucify him!" the mob shouted back.

"I am innocent of this man's blood," Pilate said. "It is your responsibility." Then he brought out a wash basin and symbolically washed his hands. "Let his blood be on your hands," he said.

But can we absolve Pilate just because he was weak? After all, he signed the death warrant. And what about those Roman soldiers who actually drove the nails into his hands and feet? Then there is Judas—who betrayed him. The question remains. Who killed Jesus?

Just two weeks before he was crucified, Jesus sat with his disciples near Betharba, on the far side of the Jordan. There, while a nearby shepherd tended his flock of sheep, Jesus compared his ministry with that of a shepherd. "I am the good shepherd," he told them. "The good shepherd lays down his life for the sheep. . . . I know my sheep and my sheep know me . . . and I lay down my life for my sheep" (Jn 10:11, 14-15).

Then Jesus said something which agitated the religious Jews, and confused his followers. It was not until after his crucifixion and resurrection that they began to understand what he was talking about. Jesus said, "The reason my Father loves me is that I lay down my life—only to take it up again. No one takes it from me, but I lay it down of my own accord. I have authority to lay it down and authority to take it up again. This command I received from my Father" (Jn 10:17-18).

Who killed Jesus? The Bible says no one killed him. Rather, he voluntarily laid down his life for us. Paul sums it up in his letter to the Romans: "You see, at just the right time, when we were still powerless, Christ died for the ungodly. Very rarely will anyone die for a righteous man, though for a good man someone might possibly dare to die. But God demonstrates his own love for us in this: While we were still sinners, Christ died for us" (Rom 5:6-8).

The Romans did not take Jesus' life. The Jews didn't do it. Pilate didn't do it. Judas didn't do it.

Jesus died voluntarily. He laid down his life because he loves us.

Today, 2,000 years after Jesus was crucified on a hill just outside the city wall, the old city remains much as it was then. Filled with teeming humanity. The crossroads of the earth. The poor. The rich. People from the Middle East, from the Orient, from Europe, from the Americas . . . all come here—drawn by that strange, compelling force which draws men to God. The power of the Holy Spirit.

Despite what happened 2,000 years ago, life in Jerusalem goes on obliviously. The land beneath Golgotha—the place where he was crucified—has been paved. It is now a bus station—the heart of the city's activity. The rocks of Calvary are stained with diesel smoke. Is that a sacrilege? I think not. Rather it seems providential.

An unknown author put it this way:

"I simply argue that the Cross be raised again at the center of the marketplace as well as on the steeple of the church. I am recovering the claim that Jesus was not crucified in a cathedral between two candles, but on a rugged cross between two thieves on a town garbage heap; at the crossroads of politics so cosmopolitan that they had to write his title in Hebrew and in Latin and in Greek ... And at a kind of place where cynics talk smut, and thieves curse and soldiers gamble. Because that is where he died, Golgotha's tree; and that is what he died about.

It is there where Christ's men ought to be, and what church people ought to be about."

47

He Laid Down His Life

"... I lay down my life—only to take it up again. No one takes it from me, but I lay it down of my own accord...." (Jn 10:17–18)

BEFORE LEAVING FOR ISRAEL I had breakfast with a former priest—a man who had left the church, turned his back on his ministry. He told me he no longer believes in God.

I asked him what happened. "My center of values changed," he said honestly. "God used to be at the center of my life. But God never made me rich like I am today. Now money is the center of my life."

He had tasted God, tasted the world, and chosen the world—for you cannot choose both.

Down there, on a hill, just outside the city wall of Jerusalem, the world crucified the Son of God. Yet that execution was a result of a choice Jesus had made. Instead of choosing the world—he chose the cross. Yes, he suffered, but not out of helplessness. He was not a victim of the cross—he was victorious over the cross.

I've been up here, sitting on the parapet of the wall around the old city, since early this morning. It's possible, by paying a small fee and walking through a tiny turnstile, to climb the old stone steps which take you to the top of this ancient wall. In fact, you can walk most of the way around the perimeter of the old city on top of the wall. But I walked only to where I am now, to a place overlooking the hill of Calvary. I've been here since dawn, looking at that place, trying to let soak into my dry sponge of a brain exactly what Jesus did that morning when he laid down his life for me.

The execution of Jesus was a result of personal choice. "No man takes my life away from me," he told his disciples. "I have the power to lay it down and the power to take it again."

Does that sound strange? It shouldn't. God has given the same option to each of us. We have the power of choice. In the face of the cross, we each choose a particular way. The former priest I had breakfast with had chosen. But he chose to follow the way of the world rather than the way of the cross.

Jesus was not a victim of an evil empire. He was not broken and defeated by existing religions and political corruptions. No one killed him. He voluntarily laid down his life as an atonement for our sin.

From where I'm sitting on this piece of white granite I can see the Garden of Gethsemane on the Mount of Olives over to my right. It was there Jesus made the crucial decision of his life. As difficult as it was, he chose to go to the cross.

"The hour is come that the Son of Man should be glorified," he told his disciples. Glorified? What a mixture of terms. Didn't he mean crucified? Yet when I pause and think, I realized Jesus meant what he said. Through his death Jesus was glorified.

What does that mean? It means it was his power, not his weakness, that sent Jesus to the cross.

This morning, as I've sat here with my Bible in my lap, I've reread that story. There's one place where Jesus said he could have called upon the armies of heaven—10,000 angels—to rescue him. I used to think that meant that, unassisted, he was unable to avoid execution. That the political and religious machinery of that day was too much for him.

Not so. Jesus did not call for the armies of heaven because he didn't need them. His power alone was enough for the task. There was never a moment during that execution when Jesus was not in full control.

Deep in the heart of the city of Jerusalem, the Roman governor Pontius Pilate presided over the trial of Jesus. Yesterday I stood on the very flagstones where Jesus was standing when Pilate said to him, "Don't you realize I have power either to free you or to crucify you?"

Jesus looked him straight in the eye. "You would have no power over me if it were not given to you from above" (Jn 19:10-11).

Who does that sound like was in control?

I guess one of the hidden dreads we Christians have had is our secret fear that one day, sooner or later, evil is going to win. We live in anxiety that evil people are going to do us in, that ultimately evil governments are going to rule the world, that immorality will wipe out all decency.

Not so. We have this dread because we think the contest at the cross between Jesus and Satan was neck-and-neck ... with Satan winning momentarily. We think Jesus could have won had he called those angels, but he was too full of love. We equate a loving commitment with weakness. We westerners, in particular, think that surrendering to his enemies meant Jesus allowed his life to be snuffed out.

Up there in Gethsemane Peter drew his sword for just that reason—to defend Jesus and keep evil men from winning. But Jesus told Peter to put away his sword. Why? Because Jesus knew his time of victory—not defeat—had come. He didn't give the devil anything at the cross. He conceded nothing.

His body, not his life, was all that died and was buried in a tomb. Yet even while friends were reverently wrapping his physical body for burial, Jesus was walking through the dark regions of hell, displaying his total dominion over Satan. Even those in hell saw that Jesus was in charge. He triumphed.

In the struggle between God and Satan there has never been a time when God was not in full control. From the Garden of Eden to the resurrection—our God reigns. God not only created this world, he oversees it. He not only was witnessing what was happening at the cross, he planned it. He never abandoned his Son to the enemy . . . nor will he abandon us.

Sitting here this morning, looking at Calvary's hill, I've concluded we need to take another trip to the courthouse of this planet and read the signature on the title deed. It belongs to God. Satan has always been a trespasser on God's property.

This is my Father's world, and let me ne'er forget, That tho' the wrong seems oft' so strong, God is the ruler yet. ("This is my Father's world" by Maltbie D. Babcock, 1856-1901)

Who owned Calvary? Who grew the tree that became the wood for the cross? Who put the minerals in the earth that men mined and made into nails? Who planted the bush that grew the thorns that pierced his brow? Who gave life to men like Caiaphas the high priest, Herod the wicked king, Pilate the sniveling Roman governor?

God gave the authority in the Great Judgment Hall to declare his own death. No man took Jesus' life. He laid it down—for us. Jesus chose to walk the way of the cross.

48

Calvary

And they crucified him. . . . (Mk 15:24)

WHY DID JESUS HAVE TO DIE? Behind me is the hill called Calvary. The place of the skull. Golgotha. Today it looms over the Jerusalem city bus station. Clouds of diesel smoke disfigure its face. Below, on the street, thousands of people pass back and forth—never looking up. Vendors hawk their wares. Beggars stand with their hands outstretched. Jews, Arabs, even Christians go by this place by the thousands. But Calvary still stands—a lone monument to the most significant event in history—the crucifixion of the Son of God.

But why? Why did it have to happen? Why did Jesus have to die?

"Behold the Lamb of God," John the Baptist had shouted, pointing at Jesus who was standing quietly with the others, "who takes away the sin of the world."

How did John know? God had spoken to him. For centuries the Jews believed that only when the high priest went into the temple on the Day of Atonement—Yom Kippur—and sacrificed a lamb could their sins be forgiven.

That was the old covenant. Now God was making a new covenant with his people. Jesus, the Son of God—the Lamb of God—was going to die, once and for all. By his sacrificial death not only was the penalty paid, but he would break the chains of death through his resurrection and open a way that all of us might have eternal life.

Last night I sat up for a long time, going back through some of the passages I had marked in my Bible across the years. I noticed, in the Book of Romans, the first verses I had marked were what some call the "Roman Road to Salvation." In those verses Paul outlines why Jesus died here on this hill.

1. "All have sinned and fall short of the glory of God" (Rom 3:23). Jesus was the only sinless man. The Bible taught that the sacrifice on the day of atonement had to be a "lamb without blemish." Jesus was the only one in all history qualified to die for our sin—for he was sinless.

2. Then Paul gives us bad news and good news. The bad news is this: "The wages of sin"—the price we pay for rebelling against God—"is death." But then he adds the good news: "The gift of God is eternal life in Christ Jesus our Lord" (Rom 6:23).

3. Why did Jesus have to die? Paul answers it in the fifth chapter of Romans. "You see, at just the right time, when we were still powerless, Christ died for the ungodly. Very rarely will anyone die for a righteous man, though for a good man someone might possibly dare to die. But God demonstrates his own love for us in this: While we were still sinners, Christ died for us" (Rom 5:6-8).

4. So, what do we have to do to receive this wonderful eternal life provided for us by the death of Jesus Christ? Paul provides the answer. "If you confess with your mouth, 'Jesus is Lord,' and believe in your heart that God raised him from the dead, you will be saved. For it is with your heart that you believe and are justified, and it is with your mouth that you confess and are saved" (Rom 10:9-10).

That's why Jesus died. To open the door back to God. All we have to do is let him be Lord of our lives. How is that done? By believing in your heart that he really did rise from the dead.

How can you know that?

Well, for one thing, because it's historical fact. Just a few yards from where I'm standing, just to the left of the summit of Calvary, is an empty tomb in a garden—a testimony of the awesome power of God over death.

Equally important is the testimony of millions of men and women whose lives have been changed by the living Christ. I am one of those. There was a time in my life when I was heading for certain destruction. Then I prayed—and asked the living Christ to take control. He did. Oh, how he did! Ever since then I have been ruled by Jesus Christ.

It's a strange but beautiful story. Strange, because it had its origin in the horrible death of the sinless Son of God. He came to give this world nothing but love and mercy—and the world rejected both him and his message—crucifying him on this hill.

Beautiful, because out of that death came life for all mankind—including me. For that I am eternally grateful.

49

Resurrection

> ..."Why do you look for the living among the dead? He is not here; he has risen! ..." (Lk 24:5–6)

IT'S BEEN MORE THAN A DOZEN YEARS since my daddy died. Yet, on this early Easter morning, as I sit in this quiet garden in Jerusalem, looking through the trees and flowers at the open tomb, I want to write it down.

We had just come in from the Sunday church service and the phone was ringing. It was my mother.

"Daddy B has just gone to be with the Lord." He was 87.

My wife and I left our Sunday dinner on the table and walked back out the door. It was a thirty-mile drive down the east coast of Florida to the old home place in Vero Beach where I had been born and raised.

Twenty-five years earlier, kneeling in his orange grove behind the house during a time of personal crisis, Daddy had given his heart to Jesus Christ. Though he had been a churchgoer all his life, he had never had a personal relationship with Jesus. That is, until that morning in the orange grove. His life goals and his personal desires instantly and radically changed. He immersed himself in the Bible. Israel became his second home, even though he never visited it.

I remember one Easter, the year after he became a Christian. I was home from college for spring break. Daddy was so eager for me to know Jesus the way he knew him. We sat on the front steps and I listened as he described the Sea of Galilee, the mountains around it, the fishing boats, the little villages, and how Jesus had—from that place—taught the world about the kingdom of God.

"I'll never get to walk where Jesus walked," he told me. "But one day you'll go to Israel. You'll get to see it for yourself and you'll bless many others as you describe it to them. But when you go, remember this: it's not walking where Jesus walked that really counts. It's walking with him day by day that makes the difference in life."

Daddy believed Jesus was still alive. "Because Jesus lives," he told me, "all who believe in him will live too—even after their bodies die."

The week before Daddy died I sat on the side of his bed, listening as he quoted Longfellow.

Tell me not, in mournful numbers,
Life is but an empty dream!—
For the soul is dead that slumbers,
And things are not what they seem.

In his poetic way he was telling me he was about to die. It didn't seem to bother him. He believed death was a beginning—not an end.

I believed that too. At least I wanted to. But as I drove in silence, Job's question kept swirling through my mind. "If a man dies, will he live again?" It's a question we all ask when death strikes.

Mother had said, "Daddy B has gone to be with the Lord." How did she know? How does anyone know where you go when you die? What's to prove you're not like ants stepped on by kids, or like leaves burned in the fireplace?

We pulled up in the carport and I went back to his room.

His body was on the bed, the thin, tan blanket pulled up over his chest. His mouth was partially open, his arm hanging at an awkward angle off his bed. I knelt beside him and could almost hear Longfellow again, echoing in the empty room:

> Life is real! Life is earnest!
> And the grave is not its goal;
> Dust thou art, to dust returnest,
> Was not spoken of the soul.

Caressing his hand, I remembered him telling me how he had caught me with those hands when I had been born at home. For the first time, I cried.

I stood, looking out the window at the Florida he loved so much. He used to call it "eternal springtime," reminding us of the harsh winters back in Indiana. Then in silent words he spoke to me. I've reexamined that sacred moment many times since then. Was I imagining? Was I wanting to believe so desperately that I had just made it up? No, for when I mentioned it to my wife, she had sensed virtually the same thing.

"You think Florida is beautiful?" he said. "What you see out the window, son, is nothing compared to what I see."

There was more, but it's too personal to relate here. The important thing was this: my doubt was gone. In its place was hope. Not the kind of hope that says, "I hope he's still alive." Rather the biblical kind—the kind that Paul talked about in the Book of Hebrews: "We have this hope as an anchor for the soul, firm and secure."

Jesus' open tomb is God's message of hope to each of us. "If a man dies, will he live again?" that early Jew asked. Another Jew answered with more than words. In this place, this garden tomb in Jerusalem, Jesus answered with his life.

That early morning so many years ago, the grieving women who loved Jesus so much came to anoint his body with spices. But the huge stone had been removed from the entrance to the cave. The tomb was empty. Peering inside they were startled by a bright, shining angel sitting on the ledge where they had laid him.

"Why do you look for the living among the dead?" the angel asked gently. Then he made the proclamation that changed all history. Forever. "He is not here. He is risen."

Because He lives, you and I shall live also.
He is risen!
He is risen indeed.

50

Wait for the Promised Gift

"But you will receive power when the Holy Spirit comes on you. . . ." (Acts 1:8)

URING HIS MINISTRY on earth Jesus spent a lot of time with his disciples—that small group of men and women who followed him, who were committed to him as their spiritual mentor. While the Bible writers concentrate on the twelve *men* who were later called apostles, there were also a number of women who were close to him: Mary and Martha from Bethany—in whose house he stayed when he came to Jerusalem; Joanna; Mary Magdalene; plus a number of others who are unnamed.

Yet it was the twelve men, most of whom were Galilean fishermen, to whom he imparted most of his teaching.

After Jesus had died, his followers, men and women, removed his body from the cross and brought it to a new tomb, a cave in the side of a hill just a few yards from Golgotha. The tomb was furnished by a wealthy man named Joseph from the nearby town of Arimathea. While not one of Jesus' close disciples, Joseph was like many in Israel who believed Jesus was the Messiah—God come in the flesh.

But it did not end there. Every earthly funeral is finished when the empty hearse pulls out of the cemetery, leaving the casket in the earth. Not this one. On the third day angels came to Jesus' grave. They rolled back the giant stone which blocked the entrance. Then the Holy Spirit, in a rush of power greater than all the electrical surges in the world, entered the tomb and filled the dead body of the Son of God with life. And Jesus, rising from the dead, walked out of the grave and into the hearts of all who will accept him as Lord and Savior.

Fifty days later Jesus stood very near where I am this morning on the Mount of Olives. Turning to his disciples, he commissioned them with words so familiar you and I have memorized them: "Go and make disciples of all nations, baptizing them in the name of the Father, the Son and the Holy Spirit, and teaching them to obey everything I have commanded you."

But there was one final thing. I can't believe how many churches, how many Christians, omit it. I'll not try to analyze why. Maybe because it is so important that Satan has blinded us from it. Maybe it is because it carries with it the threat of a changed life. Maybe because this one element is the thing which involves us in Jesus' ongoing ministry—something we're not quite prepared to do. Whatever the reason for its omission, I am convinced that aside from the actual atonement at Calvary and his resurrection from the dead, this is the singular most important thing Jesus ever said.

Looking at his loyal friends he said, "Do not leave Jerusalem, but wait for the gift my Father promised, for in a few days you will be baptized in the Holy Spirit."

Then Jesus added, "You will receive power, when the Holy Spirit comes upon you, and you will be my witnesses in Jerusalem, and in all Judea and Samaria, and to the ends of the earth."

Then, suddenly, he was gone.

The rest of the New Testament is either recordings of how Jesus' disciples were used by the Holy Spirit to conduct his continuing ministry, or as instruction to us on how to do it ourselves.

His followers, filled with hope and anticipation, gathered in an upper room in Jerusalem to pray—waiting to see what would happen. The story is told in Acts 2. "Suddenly a sound like the blowing of a violent wind came from heaven and filled the whole house where they were sitting.... All of them were filled with the Holy Spirit and began to speak in other tongues as the Spirit enabled them."

The Holy Spirit not only filled those 120 believers, but he continues to fill all of us who believe across the centuries—giving us the same power and authority that Jesus had while he was on earth. The night before he was crucified, Jesus told his followers: "Greater things than I have done, will you do—because I go to my Father . . . and if I go to the Father I will send the Holy Spirit . . ."

The story did not end with the crucifixion. Nor does it end with Easter. It only begins there for, like those early disciples, each of us has been commanded to seek and receive the baptism of the Holy Spirit so we might be empowered, as those early Christians were, to go into all the world and tell others about our risen Lord.

Miracle Power

by Jamie Buckingham

There are no limits to what God may choose to do to - and through - us.

'Miracles should be the norm in the life of the Christian', insists Jamie Buckingham. 'Because we are constantly stumbling through a dark world, we need God to guide our footsteps, giving us the ability to walk supernaturally.

'That means miracles. But God is not restoring miracles to the church. They've been there all along. He is simply waiting for simple people who will step forward in faith and expect God to use them.'

Jamie Buckingham has experienced many miracles himself in the course of his long ministry. His study of miracles in the New Testament and today - miracles of healing, power, provision and hope - is designed 'to stimulate you, excite you and hopefully to convince you that the miracles of Jesus were not for yesterday - they are for today.'

Jamie Buckingham is the author of many books including *Risky Living*, *Where Eagles Soar* and *The Truth Will Set You Free, But First It Will Make You Miserable*.

Kingsway Publications

Appointment in Jerusalem

by Lydia Prince
as told to her husband Derek Prince

The true story of a schoolteacher who dared to be led by the Holy Spirit . . . and of the city where God has hidden the key to the future.

Lydia had everything. Education, money, social position . . . a fulfilling professional life as head of a department at her school . . . a luxurious apartment with a devoted maid to care for it . . . parties, dancing, admiring friends, expensive clothes . . . and a proposal of marriage. What strange series of events led her to abandon all this and journey alone and penniless to an alien land where she would experience almost daily danger?

Appointment in Jerusalem is the unforgettable true story of a twentieth century woman who dared to take the Bible at its literal face value and in so doing discovered what many seek but few ever find. Joy. Peace. Perfect security — no matter how desperate the external condition of her life.

Lydia Prince resided for twenty years in Jerusalem where she mothered scores of abandoned Jewish and Arab children and witnessed the birth of modern Israel. At the close of World War II, she married Derek Prince and the couple had nine adopted daughters from Jewish, Arab, British and African backgrounds.

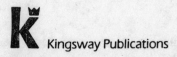

Kingsway Publications

More than a carpenter

by Josh McDowell

What makes Jesus so different?

He may have been a good man, even a great teacher—but what has he got to do with our lives today?

Josh McDowell thought Christians must be out of their minds. He put them down. He argued against their faith. But then he discovered for himself the truth about Jesus, and experienced his life-changing power.

Here he brings answers for those who are as sceptical as he was—answers for those who have doubts about Jesus, his deity, his resurrection and his claim on their lives.

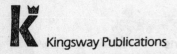

Kingsway Publications

The Uniqueness Of Israel

by Lance Lambert

Woven into the fabric of Jewish existence there is an undeniable uniqueness. Israel's terrain, her history and chief city, all owe their uniqueness to the fact that God's appointed Saviour for the world was born a Jew. His destiny and theirs are for ever intertwined.

There is bitter controversy over the subject of Israel, but time itself will establish the truth about this nation's place in God's plan. For Lance Lambert, the Lord Jesus is the key that unlocks Jewish history. He is the key not only to their fall, but also to their restoration. For in spite of the fact that they rejected him, he has not rejected them.

K
Kingsway Publications